STEAM·TRAINS

OF THE WORLD

STEAM·TRAINS
OF THE WORLD

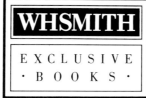

WHSMITH

EXCLUSIVE
·BOOKS·

Steam Trains of the World
was conceived, designed and edited by
Labyrinth Publishing S.A., Chamerstrasse 50, 6300-Zug, Switzerland.

First published in Great Britain in 1987
by W.H. Smith Publishing Ltd.

ISBN 999799991

Produced in Barcelona, Spain, by Reprocolor Llovet, S.A. Printed by Norial, S.A.
Color separation by Studio Leonardo Fotolito s.l.r., Italy.
Typesetting by Linograf, Florence, Italy.
First edition.

D. L. B. 35511-87

CONTENTS

I N T R O D U C T I O N

Ex-GWR 2-6-2T number 6164
at work on one of Britain's preserved railways.

BACK IN 1969 I gave up a promising career in marketing in order to undertake the task of documenting the history and existence of steam locomotion – much to the horror of my family and friends. I started off without a camera, without money and with no experience of photography whatever. The company I worked for told me I would be back within six months – and this was seventeen years ago.

My feeling was that someone had to do the job – the age of steam was drawing to a close throughout the western world, it was only a matter of time before the Third World countries would follow suit and the entire dynasty of steam locomotion would disappear from the planet.

Steam traction in America was run down at a horrific rate, while in no more than twenty years Britain destroyed almost thirty thousand steam locomotives, including some six hundred different types. Nobody had expected such a rapid change – even experienced railway writers had predicted that steam traction would at least last through into the twenty-first century. The modernization plan was only announced in Britain in 1955 and by August 1968 the fires were dropped for the last time and the steam locomotive became extinct in the land of its birth – in just fourteen years a substantial revolution had occurred.

Steam traction was the motive force behind the Industrial Revolution – allowing it to gather at a tremendous momentum – and perhaps also Britain's greatest gift to the world. Britain built an enormous proportion of the steam engines that were exported throughout the rest of the world, and everywhere the engines went the Industrial Revolution spread. It was this spread of technical knowledge which formed today's world.

The very early days of my determination to complete a record on film of the remaining steam were tough – with support from my friends, no initial income and living only in a small studio apartment. But as time moved on, lectures and shows of the images I had collected brought greater success and allowed me to travel more widely in my search. Additionally, living in England permitted me to have ready access to the foundry records which told me where to begin my hunt for engines that were exported to the ends of the world.

The next most interesting question that I was able to answer over the last years was why steam locomotion was run down at all.

Here again, Britain might be a good example, for when this country was at its supreme in the world's industrial innovations, coal was plentiful and of good quality, whereas after World War II oil became plentiful and cheap, and coal was already on the wane, both in quantity and quality. Poor coal will not drive the best of steam locomotives; a factor in the advent of dieselization.

It was also said that steam was dirty, unhealthy and created foggy atmospheres. The industrial clean-up that came after World War II brought with it a preoccupation with tidying up the general social order: clearing slums, rehousing, disposing of slag-tips; there was a general run-down on the kind of work that was regarded as dirty. During the 50s it was also said that labor for steam locomotive work could not be found – that the younger men did not want to be involved in such activity. Whether this was simply propaganda, I don't know; it was my experience that thousands of steam workers started at the age of fourteen and worked their way up the steam engine ladder until retirement age at sixty-five – indeed some of them are still around now, in their nineties.

But the most significant reason for steam's departure must have been the setting up of the diesel industries. Once the investment had taken place and the diesel plant was there to build the engines, it was the task of those who had made the initial investment to persuade railway administrations to get rid of their steam locomotives – a natural practice of good business. Additionally, of course, there came the birth of the newest form of money-making, a scheme which had never existed before in any force and certainly not in the steam world – that of planned obsolescence: you built the diesel in such a way that after a fixed period of time it would need repairing or replacing. Engines were no longer created at their very best – fit to last a century.

The factories that built diesel prefered to specialize; it was not part of their plan to diversify their plant. Drivers and engineers could work in better conditions – no windy draughts, no coal dust. If they could work this way, why should they work any other way?

With the death of steam locomotive in America and Britain, came also the closure of hundreds of miles of track which in turn opened the flood gates for the building of roads and the development of the motor car. The result was, on one side, congested and overworked roadways, and on the other, world railway systems, poorly and inefficiently run. Railway had effectively to be redeveloped from scratch and the work still goes on – somehow a strange sequence for world authorities to take up: the destruction of one effective railway system in order to build another not so good.

Another factor in the evolution of the locomotive was the various schools of design. The main ones are the British, the American, the German, the French and the Austrian – five schools with fairly distinct characteristics. The others that existed throughout the world were less innovative and more derivative. A separate order of locomotives might be regarded as those built for war. These six categories were the fundamentals of locomotive design and formed the world's arrangement of steam on wheels.

We can start with the British – esthetically pleasing, with clean lines and elegant shapes – with the ideal of this design form reaching its peak at the end of the nineteenth century, with chief mechanical engineers in Britain going to tremendous lengths to retain this purity of appearance. These engines were exported all over the world, design and all, whether it suited conditions and terrain or not. Foundries such as Beyer Peacock in the north of England, who built over seven thousand locomotives, the North British Locomotive Company in Glasgow, Scotland, the second largest foundry in the world, and many other, all great builders, created the steam that would help create the world. And although most of these foundries are now totally closed down, many of the engines they built sometimes over a hundred years ago are still functioning. Such craftsmanship and workmanship does not exist in any form today.

This British school is no doubt matched on the other side of the Atlantic in America by machines that developed in a different way because of the terrain they had to cross and the demands made upon them. Very quickly they outpaced those of British design and once the 4-4-0 stage had been passed in America, the locomotive there really took off in terms of size. By the early years of the twentieth century enormous creations were running, with two cylinders, wide fire boxes that spread out over the rear axles and bar frames as opposed to the plate frames of the British. There was also an immense generic similarity – just as the old 4-4-0s were generic in their appearance, so did the American steam locomotive have a tremendous family likeness. They were designed by committees from amongst the larger companies, whereas in England the design was always undertaken by a large number of small private companies working with their own workshops. Baldwins, and Lima of Ohio, in America, were very large companies who serviced all the railway systems throughout the nation and therefore created a much greater similarity amongst the engines that ran the United States' railroads.

But with all its rugged simplicity the American design did not really make as great an impact on the world as the British did until the beginning of the twentieth century. This was largely because American builders were far too busy coping with the demands of their own land – with the extending of track and the perfecting of their foundries – to find time to consider exports. And of course there was no imperial motivation in America as there was in Britain.

But after the beginning of the twentieth century the emphasis changed dramatically; something of a saturation point was reached in America, with the large capacity for building running out, and the Americans were putting on an incredible drive to sell their exports, including steam locomotion, to the rest of the world. Countries like Africa, India, Russia, South America

needed tough and rugged engines that were built in a country that knew what tough meant – America, naturally. The British fine-art versions were not always ideal if an authority wanted to crash through jungle or across mountain terrain.

The British and American companies were competing for export sales and the North British Locomotive Company was created to fight this battle using more conveyer belt methods than ever before.

The American steam locomotive was never to be out of the spotlight thereafter and many of the engines depicted in this book are those that have remained in many parts of the world till today.

Germany's growth was somewhat less dramatic – as a major industrial nation, though, Germany was building steam locomotives right from the start. The style was more towards the British than the American, and might be called the masculine version of the softer British design. The engines were larger, especially in the later years, though never as large as the American locomotives. Germany did not export to the extent of the American or British companies, and the largest part of her dispersal was as a result of the two world wars, both wars producing their own basic designs – with for example the 50 class 2-10-0 as a design creating some six thousand locomotives.

The Kriegslokomotiv of World War II later became one of the major standards of the rest of Europe. As in America, there was no empire to export to, though throughout the twentieth century Germany did export the smaller industrial engines to many other countries.

Design was not diverse in Germany, with the larger companies supplying both the home and export engines. Unlike Britain, both Germany and America built their locomotives with the aid of independent and large foundries, whereas in Britain the railway companies themselves had their own foundries.

The next school is the French, which in order of importance comes after

(Left)
Steam traction does not have to be dirty. When the work was formerly done, pride in the job meant that there were few things cleaner than a steam locomotive.

(Opposite)
A Stanier Black 5-4-6-0 in preserved form working a main line special in Britain.

the German. France did have colonial territories into which "homespun" designs were sent. Many years ago, countries such as North Africa and Indo-China received France's very distinctive designs, but the school which was once wide spread, is now close to extinction. This is partly because, compared to other countries, the majority of her engines stayed at home.

Austria, in the form of the Austrian Empire, was even more localized – producing from the Austrian State Railway engines that were inherited largely because of the carving up of the Empire. When the new boundaries had been formed, countries like Yugoslavia, Czechoslovakia and Hungary took on the Austrian designs and started to build their own engines based on them.

Russian steam was basically derived from American design, and they have built from the same source until the end of steam.

Japan is another major locomotive-building country which also took its early design from America. China, however, forms a unique area of steam-engine building, starting as it did, fairly late in the evolution of railways. In the early years her motive power came from all the main schools of design, but once the Japanese took hold in Manchuria, the main design form became American, imported by the Japanese. China then began to build identical designs and today it is evident that the major part of Chinese railway is still greatly dominated by designs from the United States. It is clear therefore that the major schools of design are distinctly distributed throughout the world.

The remaining continents of Africa, South America and India took nearly everything from the main design areas.

Engines from the two world wars were generally austere, stripped of all adornments and reduced to the essential features. They were built tough and hardy – the S160s of World War II, the famous Hunslet Austerities from Britain, the Pershings of World War I, the German Kriegslokomotiv, the Feldbahn (with three and a half thousand built by eighteen different builders and forming one of the standard industrial locomotives of the twentieth cen-

tury) – these and others take a design form of their own, created from the theater of war.

The builders of these engines who were unable to adapt their operations to diesel, also went out of business at the death of steam.

Now it seems worthwhile to briefly cover the main belts of steam around the world and their design sources.

We start with Africa where the main involvement came from Britain. The Garratt, probably the most important design in the evolution of locomotion, is a main form on this continent. These engines set the whole trend for steam throughout Africa and Zimbabwe where engines are still being renovated. Sudan locomotives were recently overhauled by Britain as part of the "Band-Aid" program.

India contains the greatest diversity of steam and probably the area where the greatest diversity can be found. This part of the world makes tremendous use of their steam locomotion with a very dense use of railway still in service, with British workmanship seen both in industry and passenger railways. American influence, of course, is also very great here.

In Europe, very little steam traction survives, with the exception of Poland, East Germany and Yugoslavia, all three countries dominated by German and old Prussian and Austrian influences. The rest of the European countries are largely finished with steam, with a few scattered exceptions in Spain, Italy and Hungary where it is still used mainly for standby work. In the Middle East there is only Syria operating German locomotives.

Turkey hangs on with some superb German designs, very often dating back to Prussian times, even though the country's administration has been trying to "modernize" for years.

In Russia there were tens of thousands of steam engines right up to the late 50s. But railway modernization has taken over and is considered important. Nevertheless there are still steam engines around, though most will not be seen or documented as the Russians do not encourage foreign interest in their railway network.

The high spot of steam is in China, still building engines at the rate of one a day all year round from at least three separate works. They have the coal, the water and the labor, and can build steam locomotives for one-eighth of the price of diesel and the engines last ten times longer. They even put in research to improve the work of steam and proudly announce their determinations in this field of industry. There is some likelihood of new designs in China which could increase the general life of steam.

Of course the whole of North America and Canada are completely steam-free. America was the very first country to annihilate steam from their railroads and convert to diesel.

A fairly large number of steam engines survive in Latin America except that the areas where these examples can be found are often difficult to locate and arduous to reach. Australia followed British traditions for many years, as did New Zealand, but both are now devoid of steam. South-East Asia is in decline, with working museums dying slowly. Only German industrial engines work in any number in the Javan sugar plantations. Negros Island in the Philippines contains much American steam, together with North Korea and Vietnam which are still also running a good variety of steam traction. Nothing happens in Japan, although they disposed of it fairly late.

Cuba, however, still displays a considerable and exciting American steam heritage – much of it built in the traditional American design in the sugar fields.

A fairly rash "guestimate" of operating steam engines throughout the world would seem to amount to about thirty thousand. The steam locomotive was such a resilient force that it is not surprising that it does not die so easily, and although most of the world's major countries have done their best to dispose of this powerful mechanism and dynasty of travel, it has not proved possible to get rid of it totally in such a short time.

Finally, what is steam actually doing around the world today? It has to be said that the majority of it is involved in the hard slow-hauling, humdrum work. Speeds of steam usage over sixty miles per hour can be found only in China, India and Poland. The majority of other work is mostly within industrial areas that do not need to move so fast, such as docks, sugar plantations, iron mines, factories where heavy materials need to be moved – these are the main areas where steam is still in regular usage. The high speeds that used to be achieved of over one hundred miles per hour, cannot be found anywhere in the world.

Passenger main-line, suburban and other passenger railway is now sparsely serviced, and even the shunting work of industrial and mixed traffic work is done by locomotives that are former freight engines downgraded for the task. In Cuba, for example, some old American passenger engines are in operation on sugar plantations, but not in the main areas of shunting work. Two and a half thousand ton trains can still be seen in Cuba and to a lesser extent in South Africa, hauled by the famous QJ engines of the past.

But remembering the hundred of different design types there once were, it is not just the diversity that is disappearing. The overall variety of traction is also vanishing. By the twenty-first century there is likely to be only a small variety of standard types anywhere. Added to that, the general richness of steam is also diminishing. In China for example, some four and a half thousand engines are QJs, two thousand are JFs, fifteen hundred are SYs and another fifteen hundred JSs – that's nine thousand five hundred engines out of the total eleven thousand engines in China. The degree of standardization speaks for itself.

Water troughs, banking, smoky sheds, and the great tapestry of evolution within the steam world – all these things are rapidly disappearing everywhere across the globe. Multi-cylinder engines with their musical sounds, are all gone. The tradition of naming engines has almost completely died out. These are just a few of the distinct characteristics of steam locomotion that gave it its unequalled magic – soon to be consumed within the dull plod of standardization.

And last of lasts, I will just mention the extremes of steam – the largest, the smallest, the oldest and the newest locomotives in existence.

The oldest is a pair of Sharp Stewart 0-4-0 tender engines built at the company's Manchester, England works in 1873. Two of these locomotives survive on India's sugar plantations – one hundred and fourteen years old.

The newest are the latest batch of Chinese QJ 2-10-2 and JS 2-8-2s, being currently built.

The biggest left in the world are the Chinese QJs, the South African Railway's 25 class 4-8-4 which tip the scales at two hundred and thirty tons in full working order. And the smallest must be some of the tiny fireless engines which are like thermos flasks on wheels and abound in industrial areas – paper mills or explosive factories – where fire sparks would be hazardous.

And so, as the world slowly finds ways to bring the whole steam locomotive era to an end, the collectors and archivists, the train spotters and enthusiasts continue to log and record the biography of the remaining engines. One day there should be sufficient evidence of an era that came and went in the space of just two centuries and transformed the world. I, for one, am pleased to have given up that marketing career to devote my life to the task and I hope that the vast number of recorded examples I have managed to gather will give pleasure to many people in the years to come.

I

UNITED STATES

The Central Pacific's "Jupiter," now on show at the Golden Spike National Historic Site in America.

THE STEAM LOCOMOTIVE arrived in America with sufficient force and perfect timing to do precisely the job needed for an emerging nation with a considerable task to perform.

America was not the first to develop steam locomotion – that had been the privilege of the English – but in the burgeoning states of America the problems that this monster of industrial development faced were far greater and more dramatic than the British pioneer engines were required to surmount. America was a vast, untouched landscape, with distances that no "civilizing" nation had previously encountered, and the terrain itself was more varied and less tamed than anywhere in the world at that time.

For adventurers, engineers, surveyors and financiers, the building of the American railroad system was to be the most exciting project in the history of the world.

Apart from the natural boundaries, such as the Allegheny Mountains – the range that hid the East Coast from the rest of accessible America – the incredible rivers such as the Mississippi that rushed across the country from south to north, and the astonishing distances that had to be covered, there were also other major obstacles to steam locomotion. One of the most potent of these was the American Indian who was, over the next half century, responsible for major loss of life amongst the new white population. The stories told of the "Old West," seen now on television and movie shows across the world, may be hard to verify in fact; but scalpings and murders were commonplace as the track workers from Ireland and China made their drive to put down the way for the iron horse.

For the old wagoners, canalmen and riverboatmen, there was also no great attraction in the coming of steam. They had all made their uncertain way across the country prior to the beginning of steam locomotion in the early 1800s, building homesteads and trade along the river banks and on the prairies, much of which would be swept away in the mid-1800s.

One of the most popular and successful vehicles to set this national force in motion was an American type 4-4-0, the definitive early form which first appeared during the 1830s, when much of the early pioneering track was well underway. The most famous example of this locomotive was called the

The "Daniel Nason" is one of the oldest surviving American steam locomotives, being the last remaining example of the "Dutch Wagon" practice where the steam cylinders were inside the loco frame – very popular before the Civil War.

(Left)
Buster Keaton in his movie *The General* made great fame of an engine that saw American Civil War drama when Union soldiers hijacked an example of the "American" and used it to fight the war.

A former San Luis Valley Southern Railroad 3ft gauge 2-8-0 built in 1890 – seen here in its Denver and Rio Grande Western Railroad guise as C-28 class at the Colorado Railroad Museum near Denver.

A Rio Grande Southern 3ft gauge 4-6-0 which once worked the Florence and Cripple Creek Railroad. Built in 1899, she is seen here at the Colorado Railroad Museum near Denver.

"Loco 999" established a world speed record on May 10, 1893, which it held for twelve years, when it hauled the Empire State Express at 112.5 MPH on a run west of Batavia, New York.

"General," built by Thomas Rogers of Paterson, New Jersey. The type formed the most numerously-ìbuilt of all the engines in this great growing country. Rogers incorporated the latest of Stephenson's developments – a gearing system that permitted more than the "full forward" and "full backward" movements, giving the opportunity to use the steam power to its complete extent. Additionally, the new design brought improved features, such as the provision of adequate space between the cylinders and the drive wheels, thus reducing the maximum angularity of the connecting rods and therefore the up-and-down forces of the slide bars.

In the rugged and varied lands of the Americas, flexibility was needed on curves, and the slightly later versions of the General contained side movement on the leading "trucks" or "bogies," producing a greater facility to handle curves at speed. The engines, of course, by then burned wood, and within this series there were a number of different devices for stopping the resulting sparks that tended to set fire to anything and anyone along the track.

Such was the popularity and building system of these engines, that any railroad company ordering them would simply fill in a form giving their choice of specifications and additional features and send it to one or other of the manufacturers, almost like buying a motor vehicle today. In these early days of US pioneering, the "extras" available were many and varied, with beautiful adornments such as brass name-plates and fancy trim. But as the competition increased, and the financial restrictions of the latter part of the nineteenth century grew, the "American" became the "American Standard" – which had a tougher style with less trim and with more severe lines. It was a locomotive type which nevertheless sold more than twenty-five thousand engines.

The General itself became famous after it was hijacked by a gang of Union soldiers who had broken through into Confederate territory during the American Civil War. Confederate reinforcements were due to arrive at Chattanooga after the Union victory at Shiloh, and the gang of soldiers who broke behind the lines planned to burn a huge trestle bridge at Oostanaula, using the General to get them there.

The Union force, twenty in number, hijacked the train while passengers were taking their breakfast at a depot, and steamed off down the one-way

Preserved USA steam in the form of a 4-6-0, formerly of the Northwest Pacific Railway.

A handsome high-wheeled Pacific now in retirement from the Texas State Railroad.

The world famous "Edaville" No. 7 – forerunner of so many different engines – preserved now in museums round the world. A 2-4-4T on the Bridgton and Saco Railroad, built by Baldwin in 1913.

Coal hauling through snowy landscapes in the US was a common enough scene throughout American history – the only thing missing now would be the vast plumes of smoke.

The Denver and Rio Grande Western Railroad K-36 class 2-8-2 at the midway station of Osier on the Cumbres and Toltec Scenic Railroad from Chama in New Mexico to Antonito in Colorado.

track, not least of their problems being the likelihood of other trains coming the other way! The General eventually ran out of steam, and the soldiers disappeared into the woods, nearly half of them eventually captured and shot. But the whole event proved the locomotive to be an incredible force in the first major war to be fought using steam locomotion. At points during the chase for this small part of the war, the locos involved traveled at speeds in excess of sixty miles per hour, considerably more than the normal velocity, which averaged out at around twenty-five miles per hour.

"America built the railroads and the railroads built America." There can be little doubt as to the veracity of this statement of the period, for railroad development made such inroads on the human capacity for movement and the definition of territories, that never again would man break barriers like these until he reached the moon. The two most evident features of innovation in US railroad growth were in speed and size. America was always *big* and *fast!* Locomotive number 999 in 1893 established the world speed record when it pulled the Empire State Express at a reputed one hundred and twelve and a half miles per hour – a mile in thirty-two seconds – and retained the

record for no less than twelve years. "Speed fever" became the vogue in the late 1890s and on into the new century throughout the whole of civilized steam locomotion countries, but especially in America. The speed records were later proved to be a little optimistic once measurement systems were more precise, and the one-hundred-mile-per-hour claims turned out to be more like eighty or ninety miles per hour! Nevertheless, the force was there for growth and improvement, and as the fares reduced, the comforts of travel increased, and the size of the locomotives grew out of all proportion to what they had been before.

By the early 1900s the Union Pacific Railroad was running the "Pacific" 4-6-2, which weighed in at around the one-hundred-ton mark. Such engines eventually became capable of thousand-mile runs at average speeds of eighty miles per hour at high altitudes, and pulling trains weighing over a thousand tons!

And into the 1940s came the ultimate in US technological capacity – the "Big Boys" locomotives which straddled the track at weights in excess of five hundred tons, becoming the heaviest land-based vehicles in man's history.

A California Western 2-8-2
Mikado in preserved form.

Southern Pacific's 1296, one of America's hardy and powerful engines.

The Chicago, Burlington and Quincy Railroad – an O-5-B class 4-8-4 built in 1940 – at the Colorado Museum near Denver.

Denver and Rio Grande Western Railroad K-36 class 2-8-2s at Silverton, the terminus of the 3ft gauge preserved line from Durango in Colorado.

(Opposite and right)
At a busy steam shed during the latter days of steam operation in the States, showing the enormous size and power of the final stages of steam development.

In the long run the American Indian hardly had a hope of surviving in the same form in the face of such drive and determination, for not only was the steam locomotive against them, but during the same period of change came the revolver and the telegraph. The power of steam was thereby enhanced by an automatic weapon and the power to "wire" along the track in advance of the train itself. These three forces of technological change brought America into the place that it occupies today.

II

UNITED KINGDOM

(Opposite)
The LWDHAM on the Torquay Steam Line – a Great Western Railway engine, climbing from Cherston to Goodrington.

(Below)
The coat of arms of the Great Western Railway, pioneered by Brunel as the only seven-foot-wide gauge main line railway ever built.

IN CONTRAST TO the United States of America, the English approach was a more sedate progress. Given a country already in the early throes of industrial growth, the mid-eighteenth century – some eighty years before the Americas were ready to start progress in steam – saw the rapid realizations of steam power transform from inefficient pumping engines, often in use in university laboratories and just starting to be used in mining operations, being converted to the wheel and track. The name, James Watt, is synonymous with the steam condenser which was developed in the quiet provincial town of Glasgow, while Watt was instrument-maker to the University's natural philosophy department. The professor of the department asked Watt to work on the Newcomen engine which managed only a few desultory puffs. The boiler used large quantities of steam to no great effect, and Watt's task was to get the engine running continuously. It took him a year to come up with the separate condenser, which cut the consumption of steam by three quarters. A very enterprising Cornishman, Richard Trevithick, in 1804, was the first to construct a steam locomotive to run on rails. Watt's realization that steam can be drawn into a vacuum chamber and fill it, and Trevithick's ambitious refinement of that technology, changed the entire face of the world.

By the year 1811 the first signs were evident in England of an incredible progress which would eventually lead to a spider's web of railway track across the entire country. As in America somewhat later, there were those that would have prevented the steam locomotion from functioning in the manner it was due to. The canal routes across and up and down the country were well established, and the steam railway would cause hardship, not only to the canalmen, but to the workers that ran the mills which the canals served. Railway was altogether too fast for any country to absorb quickly. The first users of locomotion were of course the ones that could afford it – the "brassy" north-country mining magnates who wanted to get their coal to the ports and the other industries as quickly as they could. The majority of the early railway lines and companies were privately owned, and these massively wealthy Englishmen from Liverpool, Manchester and Leeds, sunk great

The London and North Western Railway 2-4-0 No. 790 "Hardwicke", built at Crewe in 1892.

A Great Western Railway 4-6-0 No. 7819, the "Hinton Manor" shot at Exeter St. Davids station. The engine was built in 1939.

A L.N.E.R. poster of "The Coronation," made of the former L.N.E.R. A4 Pacific 4-6-2 – the "Sir Nigel Gresley" *(opposite page)* at Bournemouth during a special rail tour in the mid-1960s. These locomotives worked the express line from King's Cross, London, to Scotland.

ROYAL
RDER BRIDGE

TOM PURVIS

"THE CORONATION"
CROSSING THE ROYAL BORDER BRIDGE BERWICK-upon-TWEED
IT'S QUICKER BY RAIL
FULL INFORMATION FROM ANY L·N·E·R OFFICE OR AGENCY

Examples of the opposites to be found in the steam engine world of the past: the Cumbrian Mountain Express in all its romantic elegance.

The last British colliery where steam traction was in regular operation – the Cadley Hill Colliery on the Derbyshire coalfield in England. The left engine is "Progress" and the right, "Swiftsure", a wartime Hunslet Austerity – with a special chimney to comply with the Clean Air Act.

(Opposite)
Former LNWR 2-4-0 Hardwicke in preserved form. During the railway races in 1895 this diminutive express engine ran the 144 miles from Crewe to Carlisle at an average speed of 67.2 MPH.

(Right)
A Hunslet Austerity, this time at the Shilbottle Colliery in Northumberland, England, photographed in January 1973.

investments into the development of this monster of contemporary growth.

In this, above all else, the British steam locomotive scene was different from that of the US. The British industrialist had plenty of money, and a relatively small country to service, while the US pioneers had very little cash and a massive land to cross. Many of the early US planners came to the UK to learn about railway, but found that the designs and the systems employed there could not be applied to the rocky terrain of the US.

By the middle of the nineteenth century, private British companies were building steam locomotives in large numbers, and once the systems were perfected, higher speeds attained, and the demand was sufficient to produce high-capacity craftsmanship, companies like Beyer Peacock – founded in 1854 – began producing a prolific number of engines. The Beyer Peacock company is a legendary British builder, and though a great deal of their output was for home use in the UK, the greater mass of what they produced went abroad. As a company, with their reliable service, high workmanship and well-known patented "Garratt principle" building, they continued

A British Industrial 0-6-0 saddle tanker named "Empress". This typical outside cylinder design was built by Bagnals of Stafford in 1954 and worked for Cadley Hill Colliery, the last coal mining operation in England to keep steam going.

successfully right through until 1966 when steam locomotion was truly finished. Such companies would employ as many as three thousand workers, and their works factories covered twenty-three acres of land site in the Manchester area. All in all the company created more than seven thousand engines. Another of the most famous companies building around the same period was Kitson and Co. of Leeds in England, established in 1835 and continuing to build steam locomotives for one hundred and three years. As with other steam builders, Kitson went into liquidation in the depression of the 1930s.

The whole steam era is a strange phenomenon if we consider how it came, increased and disappeared, in the space of one century, and what it actually did to the world. Before the end of the eighteenth century, in order to travel across even as small a country as England, the only method apart from by horse or canal – or, of course, on foot – were the stagecoaches, pre-eminent but slow. To get from London to Manchester – a distance of two hundred miles along dusty, unmade roads – a traveler could be moving very slowly for days before arriving. With the advent of the steam locomotive, suddenly

the distance could be covered in hours. Relatives could be visited every weekend, businesses could extend beyond your own town – people would travel easily, and as a result, towns expanded, grew richer and more populated. Rural areas became accessible and town dwellers could take to the coast for a holiday whereas before they might never have seen the sea in all their lives. In fact the growth of seaside towns such as Blackpool – Britain's very first holiday resort – was a direct result of steam transport.

Another interesting phenomenon was that of time itself. If a businessman needed to be at the other end of the country the following day then he had better catch the train on time: appointments made by the new telegraph system had to be kept. This meant that the time in Birmingham, in the Midlands of England, had also better be the same time as in London. Prior to railway timetables, the time in one part of the country could be as much as one hour different from the time in another – and England never had any time-zone changes like the US; it isn't big enough for that. The railway-station managers were sent the time each day by telegraph, based on Greenwich mean time, so that they could adjust their stations' clocks and be in line with the line!

A fine rural English scene with the LMS 5305 mixed traffic hauling on steep gradient – the enthusiast's delight, now long gone from the British country-side.

The "Duchess of Hamilton," one of the Stanier Pacifics, built for the LMS during the 1930s.

The picture back on page 50 perfectly depicts the end of steam locomotion in England during the 60s – the great steam sheds at Patricroft then full of engines waiting for the scrap yard. On page 51 is a low angle shot with the sun filtering through banks of cloud as the last surviving Robert Stephenson and Hawthorne 17 inch 0-6-0 saddle tanker takes a loaded train over the Whittle Colliery branch in Northumberland, England.

Opposite is a Hunslet Austerity in Northumberland, England in 1971, drawing the first train load of the day from the Fenwick Colliery. *(Right)* This picture was taken at Lostock Hall depot in Lancashire, England, on the final day of steam operation – August 1968. The last engine there, the "Britannia Pacific" number 70013 – "Oliver Cromwell" had just left the depot yard for Norwich and private ownership.

Never again would Britain be a casual country: the monster technology had begun its intrepid and unstoppable advance.

Many people at the time expected to see improvements in the efficiency and capacity of the steam engine, but never in their wildest dreams did the engine manufacturers expect diesel to emerge onto the tracks that had been so energetically laid for steam. Since the turn of the century engineers had predicted that electric traction would supercede steam – in the event it took longer than they thought. Most of the locomotive companies made still another mistake in converting their works into hydraulic-diesel manufacturing plants around the early 1930s, only to find that British Railways went for diesel-electric instead.

Such was progress that by the 1960s, virtually every single steam locomotive manufacturing plant was closed down, and the passing of the steam loco-motion era became one that we all mourn today.

III

WESTERN EUROPE

The final German steam design was the 023 class 2-6-2 seen here shortly before the end of steam.

WHEN STEAM LOCOMOTION began its life in Europe, Germany was not yet Germany but a selection of states under the Austrian and Prussian Empires, slowly emerging from the struggles that would eventually result in the "Fatherland."

Like all other growing nations, the German states met the coming of steam locomotion with skepticism, believing the speed at which the trains traveled to be actually harmful to the passengers or those watching the passing "monsters" from the track-sides! This German "delirium" may not have been so far-fetched, for there are those amongst historians who would blame the advent of industrial change, heralded by steam, for the First and Second World Wars. Germany, at least, felt a growing sense of claustrophobia as the railway tracks within the countries that lay on her borders seemed all to be converging on Berlin, bringing potential enemies too close for comfort.

WEST GERMANY

In the principal years of railway development, during the nineteenth century, each state within the coming German nation created its own railway system, both for passenger and freight purposes, and one of the major features of locomotive development that brought steam a further jump ahead occurred in Prussia. It was discovered by a Dr. Wilhelm Schmidt of the Prussian State Railways that although when steam was heated normally a certain degree of efficiency could be achieved, if the steam were heated still further – or "superheated" – the result was a far higher degree of output for the amount of steam required. The steam expanded its volume and worked better for the engine. The improvements required to fit superheaters were very costly, but the European nations were enthusiastic enough to adopt the system throughout Belgium, Switzerland, Austria and France, and during the early 20th century it spread throughout the world – yet another stage in steam speed and efficiency was reached.

It was not until 1920, after the First World War, that Germany's eight

A class 44 – an engine which derived from the famous Prussian designed G12 3-cylinder 2-10-0 – crossing the Mosel River at Bullay.

An ex-Prussian 078 class 4-6-4T banks a train out of Hor in Germany's Black Forest region.

The special effect on smoke-box doors at an engine shed, photographed in 1974.

independent state railways came together in a union, bringing life to the "Deutsche Reichsbahn" – Germany's first national railway system.

The new German railway inherited, of course, the locomotives of the former states, and the best – at least in the freight areas – were the engines that came from Prussia. The finest of these were the G12 2-10-0s, the building of which continued through until 1924, at which time more than fifteen hundred examples of these most magnificent engines were at work in Germany.

Germany, of course, required the very best and the most efficient in everything on its new unified railway, and began work on standardizing these engines for the tasks they would perform. So by 1926 a new class of three-cylinder 2-10-0s were put into service – known as the 44 class. These marvelous examples of German engineering were employed, though initially in smallish numbers, eventually to move the massive loads needed to operate Germany's effort during the Second World War, right up to 1945, when there were one thousand seven hundred and fifty in active service. The engine contained an axle-loading of nineteen and a half tons, and a tractive effort of sixty

thousand, three hundred and forty pounds – making it one of the most powerful steam locomotives in Europe.

After World War II, and the division of Germany into more than one part yet again, the 44 class locomotives could be found on both sides of the Iron Curtain along with Pacific 2-8-2s, lighter 2-10-0s and smaller classes. In the West they survived in active service until the 1970s, and in the East they may still be found today, though only in a limited number of areas.

As a matter of interest, perhaps through inadvertent justice of war, the German armies in their drive to conquer and retain France, managed to leave a number of 44s behind, these examples staying in service in France for the remaining years until finally ousted by electrification. Upon the advent of this change, the remaining of these powerhouse locomotives were moved on yet again – to Turkey, where they worked again right up until recent years.

The 44s, though always world-famous as freight locomotives, were very largely restricted to use in Germany, mostly because of their very high axle-loading. For various reasons these engines did not find their way into other European countries.

A West German class 75 in the
Deutsche Dampf Museum —
2-6-2T — no longer working.

Two magnificent engines on the Nuremberg to Amberg line in Germany – locomotive 23105 and 50 622.

A German 044 class 3-cylinder
2-10-0 in typical guise with a
heavy hopper train.

Steam traction still survives successfully today in East Germany, both on the standard gauge and on the seventy-five-centimeter gauge. An attractive and scenic example of still-running steam traction in this part of the world is at Selketalbahn, where 0-4-4-0 "Mallet" tanks are run on the meter-gauge line. This turn-of-the-century veteran pulls service trains from Gernrode to Alexisbad – a twenty-five-kilometer railway. The line from Gernrode runs to the junction at Alexisbad and then splits into two – one part climbing through glorious wooded country hills to Harzgerode, and the other part meandering through lush meadow land to Strassburg. These narrow-gauge East German steam traction lines are most popular with steam-locomotive enthusiasts, as the communist authorities permit at least a degree of photographic freedom.

The Mallet is one of today's most-loved steam engines, surviving in various parts of the world in service. Its origin dates back to 1884 when the Frenchman, Anatole Mallet, devised a semi-articulated tank engine, in which the main frames were split into two units, the rear unit rigid, and the leading one articulated. The advantage of this was flexibility over sharply curved routes, with the wheels spreading the axle load over a wide area, thus giving the engine the ability to travel over lightly laid track, pulling very heavy train loads.

The Mallet was built both in tank and tender versions, and also both on narrow and wider gauge tracks. The biggest steam locomotives of all time were built on the Mallet principle – the Union Pacific's 4-8-8-4 Big Boy Mallets weighing five hundred and twenty tons, and never exceeded in size, power or capacity; Mallet was therefore one of the fundamental forms of articulated steam locomotive.

Today, the task of the steam-locomotive enthusiast is more like that of a sleuth than a train-spotter. Finding the original engines in working localities becomes increasingly difficult as the years pass by and progress quickly snatches away opportunities to enjoy an era that is rapidly becoming confined to museums.

East Germany still forms, however, one of the best lands to achieve some success in the engine detective adventures. A fine example of still existing steam that will satisfy the most ardent enthusiast exists close to the Polish

border on a railway known as the "Muskauer Waleisebahn," which was a forestry system based on Bad Muskau. The engine run on this line was one of the last working "Feldbahn" in existence. There was a time when many of these engines worked this forestry system, but today only one remains, and it is entirely possible that the dying boiler on this marvelous engine could expire at any moment.

The railway runs along the banks of the River Neiss, which divides East Germany from Poland. The woods surrounding the track are filled with derelict workings rather like a battlefield after the war is over.

If the enthusiast finds, after reading this text, that the Feldbahn remaining in East Germany is, in fact, defunct, then the only other location where an engine of this immensely important locomotive might still be found, is in north-east Poland close to the Russian border around Bialystok where it has very recently been committed to a graveyard. It is worth giving here a brief history of the Feldbahn locomotive for its major influence on Germany's position in World War I.

The Feldbahn was the German military engine of this war, running on

A German slow train headed by a 2-6-2T class 064 on the Villingen Rottweil line.

six-hundred-millimeter tracks, and used for field operations. They were the German equivalent of the Baldwin 4-6-0 tank from America, and during the war really carried the brunt of German effort on the military railway in active service.

After the Great War they were dispersed into industry and many found their way into logging railways.

Within the Polish forests around the Russian border, only the one Feldbahn still works the log trains, all other activities now being operated by diesel engines.

The survivor is TX No. 1117 built by Henschel of Cassel in 1918. The Feldbahns were produced by eleven different manufacturers, and two thousand five hundred of them were produced by 1919. Special features included a dropped floor in the cabs so that the engine-men could stand upright. Their eight-coupled wheel base was made flexible by the use of Klein-linder axles on the front and rear to enable them to negotiate the curves and uncertainties of hastily laid military track. The weight on the axles in full working order was only twelve and a half tons. The German determination during both the

world wars produced a magnificent range of steam locomotives, all of which were built as part of the "Fatherland's" effort to dominate the rest of Europe, so that their strength and lasting workmanship was perhaps some of the greatest in the world.

The whole story of German steam came a very long way from the original fears that existed within the social states of the old, split Germany, where the public were led to believe that they might contract the most terrible delirium if they traveled on the railway at all. The outcome of German efforts over the first forty-five years of the twentieth century, resulted in their steam locomotion being relegated to the new communist split of the Berlin Wall. Today there is little left actually running, but still East Germany offers the enthusiast some satisfaction and some restricted photographic freedom throughout the country.

Opposite is a beautiful scene on the Gastein-to-Klaus viaduct in Austria – the engine is an 0-6-2T on the now defunct line.

NATIONS COME AND GO, and during much of the steam age Austria was one of the most powerful nations in Europe, with its territories spread across most of what is now Germany. The Empire's most urgent task during the middle of the nineteenth century was to connect the two sea-coasts from the Adriatic Sea to the Baltic Sea, which it saw as important for its strategic power. Right in the center of this spread of land lay the Semmering Ranges of the Alps, a mountain range that would, even today, defy the efforts of engineers. Immigrant German, Czech and Italian workers were brought to Austria to undertake the incredible task of driving a track through no less than sixteen tunnels, a hundred culverts, and over sixteen viaducts! The gradients had to be kept to a maximum of one-in-forty, and special reserve curvatures were introduced to enable the engines to surmount higher potential gradients; massive lengths of stone wall were erected in order to stop mountain sides from showering the trains with rock, and often the track needed bolstering from beneath.

AUSTRIA

During this mammoth operation, seven hundred of the unfortunate immigrant work-force died in the six years before the railway was completed.

As the Austrian Empire waned and the early twentieth century brought German domination, Austrian railways still carried steam locomotion, and one of the most popular and adaptable engines to be in service was the 629 class, first introduced in 1913 for suburban and cross-country passenger work. With a light, thirteen-ton axle load, they were ideal for almost any terrain, and continued to be built until 1927. The Nazi occupation reclassified these locomotives as 77 class, which remained their name-tag until they were finally withdrawn in the '70s.

Right at the very last of the Austrian steam-locomotive era, the innovation of the Gisel chimney was brought into production. The purpose of this was to reduce fuel consumption, as railway authorities were already becoming aware of the efficiency of steam locomotion compared with the future diesel engines already by then planned. The Gisel chimney would have been of great significance in steam traction, but during the last twenty years of the

An Austrian 0-8-0 engine on the Gmund to Grossgerungs line, photographed in 1977.

A scene on the Austrian, Jenbach, mountain railway where engines run on the "rack" lines.

A 52 class 2-10-0 descending the Semmering line – one of the world's most dramatic pieces of railway engineering, with steep gradients, tight curves and some of the longest tunneling in history.

era even the very best innovations were totally disregarded, as all energy on the railways was already moving into the "traction of tomorrow" – diesel locomotion and electric.

One of the biggest names in early Austrian railway was one that remains familiar today throughout the world – Rothschild. Solomon Rothschild was, in 1835, the very first to achieve a concession from the Austro-Hungarian Empire to build a line from Vienna northward across the Danube to Florisdorf and Wagram. The emperor of the time, Ferdinand, had only come to the throne of the Empire six months earlier, so that Rothschild's naming of the railway was clearly astute – "The Kaiser Ferdinand's Nordbahn Railway." The original name, before Ferdinand gave the concession, had been the "Vienna-Bochnia Railway," and this was hastily dropped in preference to royal identification! The intention of Rothschild was also to block the efforts of his great rival Baron Sina, and his financial backers from taking a concession on the Austrian railway potential. The first section of the railway was opened in 1837, and very quickly regular steam locomotives were in constant use, until by 1839 the line traveled a total of eighty-one miles. The en-

gines themselves were British-built, the first one used on the inauguration of the line being a "Planet" type 2-2-0 built by Robert Stephenson, who supplied a further fifteen of the engines in conjunction with another British company named Tayleur.

A 2-8-2 class 93, engine number 1414 pushes a slow train from Fratres to Schwarzenau – approaching the next station fitted with crossing points.

A typical winter drama on the
OBBs Iron Mountain Railway
in Austria showing a pair of 97
class 0-6-2Ts storming a gradient on the rack section.

An 0-8-0 on the Gmund to Grossgerungs line in Austria.

A coal burning 0-6-2T on the Austrian line from Gastein to Klaus.

On this page, a shot from the Austrian meter gauge railway and *(opposite)* an 0-6-2T class 97 on the standard gauge on what was once a rack line into the "Erzberg" mountain from which the railway derived minerals and transported them for industrial use.

When steam was originally run using these incredible engines in the Lucerne Museum, there was real drama in transport.

SWITZERLAND

SWITZERLAND was one of the very first countries to convert from steam locomotion to diesel electric, although it is more noted for electric. But during the steam era it was a significant place to be because of two major attributes – as a border country, neutral during the world wars, and for its incredible scenic qualities, namely the mountains.

In order to travel across Switzerland, it was originally necessary to take a mountain pass by horse-drawn carriage over the St. Gotthard mountains. In the surveying and engineering job of boring through the middle of nearly ten kilometers of solid rock, the railway companies had a task on their hands that no pioneers had ever encountered before in Europe. A survey system known as "indirect triangulation" allowed tunnels to be bored simultaneously from both ends, so that bearings would be taken over the passes from the approaching valleys of the mountain to be tunneled. Such bearings permitted a meeting point at the center of the tunneled mountain to be reached by the two approaching crews of workers with a deviation of only a couple of inches!

The border town of Constance, a German enclave within Swiss territory, was a spot where prisoners were often exchanged during the First World War. No one in their right minds, therefore, ever got off the Swiss steam trains at Constance, and those that did in order to stretch their legs or attempt to buy a sandwich, could quite easily find themselves – particularly if they were English – being arrested and imprisoned for the duration of the war! On the train and behind the steam you were in Swiss territory, but on the station and away from the train you could be on German territory, a potential British spy – and possibly even liable to be shot! For scenic beauty Switzerland must have been one of the great paradises of the world in which to witness the running of steam locomotion. But today, apart from tourist revival runs, there is not one puff of steam to be seen – nor has there been for many years.

(Opposite)
An original "Rigibahn" locomotive seen here on the
kind of rack and pinion line it
would have operated – at the
Lucerne Museum.

(Right)
A steam tram locomotive of the
type once running in Swiss
cities – now preserved in the
Lucerne Museum.

One of the main characteristics of the small country of Switzerland is its
reputation for precision. Swiss watches are famous the world over for their
perfection and long-lasting quality. Steam engines then, and those in working
museums now, still retain this perfection and order. The museums are well
worth the visit as they are kept in wonderful condition with the engines shin-
ing and clean, having almost the mechanical precision of a Swiss watch. In
many countries there is some sentimentality about the preservation of steam
engines – not so in Switzerland. The steam engines that have been preserved
are simply an example of what Switzerland and the Swiss consider their heritage and a normal part of their historical skill.

On the Brienz-Rothorn Bahn –
an original locomotive type,
rack rail, now at the shed in
Brienz.

An 0-6-2T, meter gauge engine on the Zillertalbahn.

A French Railways 140C class 2-8-0 – a classic type from World War I, ends its days on branch line freight duty during the 1970s.

IN TODAY'S TRAVEL-ORIENTED society, fast transport is taken for granted. France was one of the very earliest countries to adopt steam locomotion for the movement of industrial fuel, when in 1818 it sent a government surveyor of mines, M. de Gallois, to visit the mining operations in the north of England where he witnessed the Blenkinsop engines at work. His report led to the first French railway, which began construction in 1823 and was granted its building application by King Louis XVIII – King Louis XVIII survived on the French throne for just one year. Whether through French logic or some other irrational force, the lines built according to the recommendations of M. de Gallois were, for the first twenty years of their existence, only to carry trucks hauled by horses. Even the passenger carriages which eventually traveled the track in the late 1820s were drawn by horses! Locomotives only saw the light later on.

Deeper investigation into the reasons why steam locomotion took so long to catch on in France reveals a greater liking for canal travel, perhaps because

FRANCE

the gentle, floating canal boats were an excellent opportunity for fishing over the sides! It was not until 1837 that a "common carrier" railway line was opened from Paris to Saint-Germain – thirteen miles of track which during its earlier years carried anything but steam locomotion, using various other forms of traction. The whole performance of early steam locomotion, particularly in France, was surrounded by much fuss and regalia. This new capital railway was opened by Queen Marie-Amelie and her entourage in the absence of King Louis-Philippe, who had by then departed from France for reasons best known to the French. Even when the trains were running regularly, the performance and regalia continued: passengers lined up on the platform if they planned to travel first class, and upon the tolling of a bell they moved through a gate and onto the seats of the carriages. The second-class travelers remained behind another gate until the first-class passengers were well-established aboard. This segregation seems to have been part of the whole game of traveling by train – almost like a funfair activity and having little to do with the requirements of travel.

The magnificent Boulogne-Basel boat train – 141R.

Probably if the people and government of France and other countries had known exactly what steam locomotion would lead to, they would never have treated it with such respect and jollity. They clearly knew nothing of how, within the next century, it would change nations, reinforce war, and generally destroy the old gentle and languishing ways of the past.

Once aboard the trains the passengers were also looked after while in transit. Along the tracks stood specially-placed officials whose task it was to make sure that the track was safe at all points of the journey, but also "to retrieve and restore to the management such objects as travelers in their excitement or jubilation might let fall from the train!"

One of the methods employed to move the train along, where steam locomotion was not permitted, was a vacuum tube between the rails. The bottom of the motor carriage of the train had a piston hanging down which was snugly fitted into the tube with leather seals. The tube was exhausted by pumps along the way which drew out the air, and as this occurred, the piston was drawn along the tube, the leather seals opening and closing around the moving piston. Steam locomotion was far too messy, smelly and dirty, as well as dangerous, for the French. They preferred vacuum tubes, which were tremendously difficult to maintain and regularly broke down, making the journeys long and tedious. Perhaps this was the French method of putting off the inevitable day when steam locomotion would take over the railways, the people and the country.

A preserved 2-4-0 – one of the earliest forms of passenger loco-motives.

FROM THE EUROPEAN LANDS of France, we now travel far north to the cold and mountainous regions of Scandinavia, where steam encountered one major problem which one might not have imagined to be the most important in such countries. In Norway, Sweden and Finland, the unexpected problem lay in forest-fire potential through the showering of chimney sparks. And as a result, it was in these countries that the most interesting developments could be seen in spark-arresting devices – leading to some very ornate and often beautiful chimney designs.

In all the history books of steam locomotion, Italy, France and Switzerland are associated with tunneling problems, not Scandinavia – presumably because there was generally no way that tunnels were ever going to be successfully bored through mountains that just went on too long for even the best surveyors and engineers to surmount. Scandinavian railways solved the problem by going around and over the mountains, not through them! However, this resulted in the largest single difficulty in railway

NORWAY

construction in these cold countries – the actual laying of the track. This was often in far-off regions of deep mountain, with months in winter when work forces could be cut off from any civilization while they surmounted high gradients and laid track along areas that would require long periods of time to climb to great heights above sea level. The railway that still carries skiers from Bergen into the mountains of Voss and Geilo was built all the way to Oslo, and at their arrival in Voss, travelers in the early days faced a climb right up to four thousand feet above sea level at Finse. It simply was not possible for any existing locomotive to do the climb alone, and a second, huge 4-8-0, was attached at the front to haul the load to the top. Steam locomotion does not, of course, still run on regular lines in Scandinavia, but in the northern heights of Finland it is still occasionally possible to see the odd engine in reserve use. One such is the locomotive depicted in the pictures on these pages. The scene is in Rovaniemi in northern Finland, where we can see the TK3 class 2-8-0 No. 1163, one of the last survivors which worked regularly in Finland right up to 1972. In this picture it can

An engine on the Swedish Jodemans Railway in Mare-fred.

An actively preserved engine at a Norwegian railway museum.

(Opposite)
A sunset at Rovaniemi in northern Finland – one of the Finnish Railway's TK3 class light 2-8-0 mixed traffic engines moving into the depot yard after a day's tripping.

(Right)
Another scene at Rovaniemi in Finland – a TK3 class 2-8-0, No. 1163 – one of the last surviving, working engines on Finnish Railways in 1972. This one is steaming up outside the shed for snow-plough work.

be seen outside the shed steaming up for steam-plough duty. The Finns call these locomotives "Little Jumbos" because they were built for lightly laid track with an axle-loading of ten point seven tons, and could therefore travel the forty-five to fifty-pound-per-yard tracks and yet pull trains of up to eight hundred and eighty tons in weight.

The Finns have a great sense of their railway history; much has been pre-

FINLAND

served, both in museums and in running order, in addition to retaining some strategic reserves.

A Cistierna Colliery locomotive
in Spain still active today.

SPAIN IS A COUNTRY for drama and tragedy, and in steam-locomotion terms, probably one of the greatest tragedies ever to occur in the genre happened in Spain. Up to the 1950s within Spain there were literally dozens of exotically designed types, embracing thousands of locomotives running on a tremendous variety of lines. During the 1950s, with the advent of Spanish tourism and the incredible revenues it brought to the country, the Spanish authorities suddenly swept away the entire fleet in a massive and uncompromising development of their railways. In just over fifteen years, virtually all Spanish railway steam vanished as though it had never existed. The modernization to diesel happened even faster than it did in England, and everything – even engines that had many years of life left in them – was destroyed as though blown off the face of the country. One of the most prestigious and fascinating railways in the world was suddenly gone before any real film photographic memory could be compiled of it. All that remains are those maintained under Spain's fairly advanced preservation program.

SPAIN

As the picture on the following page shows, the "dust and dereliction" of Spain's determined clean sweep created a tragic end in the late sixties and early seventies. This particular picture shows the depot at Lerida, where a giant 241 F class 4-8-2 remains in abandonment in August of 1970. The 241 Fs, which were the ultimate mountain-design engines supplied to the Spanish railway system, were built by Maquinista for the RENFE during the 1950s to work the main line from Madrid to Alicanti. The locomotives were superb, heavy-hauling engines built for difficult terrain and very large loads.

Up until the 1920s Spain had imported its engines from Britain, Germany, France and Belgium, at which time it began to build its own machines. One of the most prolifically-built was the 4-8-0 type, which suited Spain's difficult terrain and the imposed restrictions on axle-loading with its good adhesion. The general policy was to run few but heavy trains so that all the engines needed to have good pulling power which had to work curvacious tracks through rough country.

There was no shortage of coal, and so these types of engine ran as ideal

(Opposite)
A composition one might entitle "Dust and Dereliction," showing the tragic end to Spanish steam in the early 1970s. The depot is at Lerida – a 241 class 4-8-2. The ultimate mountain design supplied to Spain in the mid-1940s and early 50s disappeared in a sudden clearance of steam as Spain increased her economy from tourist successes in the 70s.

(Right)
A standard gauge shunter at the Gijon dock complex in Spain.

for the country. The reasons for disposing of steam locomotion so quickly and early may have had something to do with the desire for prestige in a country which clearly derived much of its income from the traveling foreigners: appearance was everything. Today, of course, the tourist would have come to Spain simply to see such diverse and remarkable antiquities. Even so, to see what does remain of these vintage engines is still worth the journey.

An "Engerth" type locomotive on the Ponferrada to Villablino line, a few miles from Santa Maria, hauling twenty coal trucks.

PORTUGAL

PORTUGAL, LIKE SPAIN, suffered from considerable problems both in her political environment and her religious – especially during the years spanning 1930 to 1940 – the very same years that saw the peak of steam locomotion in this part of the world. The population increased and the steam locomotive had by then helped build vast complexes of railway track everywhere in Southern Europe, widening people's horizons and permitting them to increase awareness of business and leisure activities. Although countries like England, France, Germany, Austria, had a rich enough economy to make improvements, the smaller countries such as Portugal could not hope to advance so rapidly, and even if the desire to bring diesel railway to the country was there, the economy was sadly lacking then – certainly no tourist industry existed to booster the lack of export facilities, as would much later be the case.

In any event, certain factions throughout Europe did not seriously favor diesel as an alternative – or the major expenses in setting up the new electric lines, the maintenance that came with it, not to mention a new and relatively untried form of technology. The Portuguese, for one, were not ready to modernize – or, more acurately, they were too busy spending money on surviving the political growth factors.

An interesting consideration crops up throughout the whole growth of railway in the world – a consideration that is now the case in South America – when governments are in upheaval, good railways can bring votes and make better economy but somehow always seem to remain in the background until stability is maintained. In Portugal around the time when Spain was enduring the Spanish Civil War, and for the fifteen years prior, there were no fewer than eight different presidents that came and went, taking with them a total of twenty revolutions that were in their turn responsible for forty-four freshly elected cabinets – all this in decade and a half. For American or Central European political arenas, such conditions have never been experienced, even though these countries too went through the growth factors of industrial revolutions. America saw

101

(Opposite)
A full shot of an engine on the 60cm gauge mine railway system, south of Ovideo, in Spain. And *(right)* a close-up of the same engine taken in 1975.

the Civil War but managed to stabilize fairly quickly, and even the French during the early part of the nineteenth century were able to avoid such a plethora of change. The steam locomotive has done much to the world but somehow in the countries of southern Europe the effects were more greatly felt.

It may be something to do with the "latin" temperament that takes a new force like steam and uses it to create initial chaos, but in Portugal there was no doubt about the people's confusion. In any event, however, the steam engines continued to plough their way across this small country in profusion.

A prime example of an engine that we mention for the first time in this book was the 2-6-0T, which at that time was in wide use on the country's meter gauge railway track. There were three different designs still in use as late as the 1970s; unlike Spain, Portugal still had not sufficiently developed its tourism to rid itself of the steam aspect of railway transport. No less than twenty of these particular locomotives were still working at that time.

Of these twenty engines, six were built by one Emil Kessler for Portugal in 1886, making them eighty-five years old when photographed (p. 104).

A scene on the meter gauge passenger line from Pavoa to Oporto taken at Lousado.

A meter gauge suburban line service in Oporto.

(Opposite)
Hauling freight and passenger coaches east of Regua across the Douro, heading for Chaves in Portugal.

(Right)
Ten km outside Espinho, a classic little meter gauge Mallet tanker.

There is little doubt that most diesel engines would have fallen apart in less than half of this time. Steam was always built to last in all conditions and these particular engines were renowned for their strength and easy maintenance. The Portuguese gave no thought to major renovation of their steam and when finally they decided to bring some more modern equipment to the railways, the effort required to set up the diesel electric system was far greater than would have been the effort to renew or modernize their existing steam locomotion. This factor seems to be common everywhere and the considerations for disposing of steam appear to be an anathema. The result in practice is that when the railways become dieselized, they don't work so well – incidentally this is one of the reasons why many countries retain some steam to work on pick-up and repair jobs, going out to tow back the broken diesel engines. The result of poor railway is more roads, more motor cars and greater internal transport congestion. This is also only on the passenger end of the business – there is also the freight. If freight cannot be transported satisfactorily by rail then the next step is trucking – more road congestion, more pollution and more frustration. The engines in Portugal

(Opposite)
In Sernada da Vouga – a meter gauge turn-table operated by man power.

(This page)
An outside cylinder 4-6-0 in northern Portugal.

(Right)
Ponferrada to Villablino, near Santa Maria – a 2-6-0, Number 31.

(Opposite)
Engine 291 – 4-6-0.

that once carried the freight and passengers had all the vintage attributes of a fussy narrow-gauge locomotive, with giant chimneys dwarfing the small smoke boxes, ornately shaped domes, elongated front ends, outside cylinders with link-motion, square cabs, and an immense tool box on the top of the side tank with a jack positioned in front of the side tanks above the cylinders.

The delights of Portuguese steam, both on the broad and narrow gauge, attracted enthusiasts from many countries, especially as narrow gauge railways had declined drastically in Europe during the late 1950 and 60s.

Up to the mid-1970s in the north of Portugal a network of meter-gauge lines radiated from Oporto and operated a stud of Mallet tank engines, as well as the smaller, conventional tank engines – mainly of German manufacture – some of which had been in service for over seventy-five years.

This can be seen as yet another example of the incredible hardiness and reliability that cannot be equalled in any way by the modern diesel equivalent.

The condition of these old engines was also resplendent, with gleaming brass work and copper-capped chimneys, highly polished – a huge museum

(Opposite)
As recently as the 1970s, the most amazing network of meter gauge railways radiated from Oporto, the lines operated by a stud of Mallet tanks of German manufacture – some 85 years old in superb condition. The whole system disappeared in the mid-1970s.

(Right)
A train from Sernada to Aveiro, headed by a 2-6-0T, built for the Val da Vouga Railway in 1910. Here again the system disappeared in the mid-1970s.

railway, actually running, with dense services reminiscent of the nineteenth century suburban services around London – and in so small a country as Portugal. By the mid-seventies, the whole operation had totally disappeared – yet another part of evolutionary history passed into memory.

(Left)
An impressive pair of double-headed side tanks – Swiss-built – 2-6-4 on the front and a 2-8-4 on the back, hauling a north-bound train from Oporto.

(Right)
An example of an 0-4-4-0 Mallet operating from San Hora da Hora – a meter gauge system. Note the semaphor signal, the old coaching stock, and the very vintage age of the engine itself.

A Greek graveyard in the nothern part of the country – an old Austrian class 580 built for Greece in 1927. The graveyard was cut up and the contents sold in 1985.

A S ANY STEAM-LOCOMOTIVE enthusiast will know, one of the most dramatic sights in the world is that of the "graveyard." For those not familiar with the genre, the end of steam locomotion left behind a plethora of locations, many of which could once be found in Greece, where old locos were left – partly because disposing of them was difficult, but also for the spare parts' value for engines that still ran. Many of these locations were so extraordinarily emotive to all who care for steam railways that special trips were made to view what remained.

As can be seen in this dramatic first picture, the graveyard is as full of flowers and vegetation as it is laden with old rusting metal. The Thesalonika graveyard in this picture was in the northern part of Greece, and the engine depicted was built for the Greek Railway – engine number 921, Austrian class 580, by Skoda of Czechoslovakia in 1927. This particular graveyard was finally cleared and the occupants exhumed, to be cut up in 1986. The Greek railways, for example in the Peleponese Peninsular of

GREECE

Greece, was a meter-gauge railway and contained some very fine locomotive designs. The oldest of these were the Z class 2-6-0T which remained in service until the 1970s.

Within these dumps, of course, there were a variety of engines, but one of the most exciting that ended its life in Greece was a "war" engine designed under the name "McArthur" – a celebrated type built for the Far Eastern War theater as American aid. These engines were still being built after the war in 1947, on the same style, intended for the war effort and exported to Greece for service thereafter.

The McArthurs were built for the United States Army Transportation Corps for service in the Far East, and saw service in India, Malaya, Thailand, Burma and the Philippines, most being built between 1942 and 1944, when the war was at its height, by the Baldwin Locomotive Company in Philadelphia and the Davenport Locomotive Company in Iowa. The cylinders were 16×24 inches, with a boiler pressure of one hundred and eighty-five pounds and a tractive effort of 20,100 pounds.

Tithorea shed was for many years after closure a dumping ground for standard gauge steam locomotives. The engine here is a World War II S160 2-8-0, built by the American Locomotive Company in 1944 for the US Army Transportation Corps.

Within Greece it is believed that the steam locomotive dumps remained, for the twenty years after steam was replaced by diesel, because the Greek authorities still believed they might one day revive the genre in the case that war would break out with neighboring Turkey. It is a strange concept that steam locomotion has always been involved in the trials of war, and the idea of rebuilding such incredible engines during the era of space travel was still thought possible right up to 1986, when the yards were eventually auctioned and their contents cut up for scrap dealers.

For those who spend time traveling the world to view the remains of steam, Greece has always formed a rich heritage. The end of the Second World War and the remains of European steam elsewhere meant that some of the most interesting locomotives ended up in Greece. In the last years, of course, even in Greece the diesel engine has replaced everything, but still it was possible to see engines in the dumps that could not be viewed anywhere else.

One example was the 2-10-0s of Austrian proportions, built in Vienna for the railways of Greece, forty of which were delivered in 1926-27. Such huge engines were used, strangely, for passenger services. Because of difficult gra-

dients, heavy trains with sleeping cars and dining cars required these large engines. Another was the Austrian 0-10-0s, heavy freight haulers, which came to Greece from Austria between 1924-28, some fifty of them being put into traffic.

The S160 class 2-8-0s, introduced by Major Marsh for the United States Army Transportation Corps, could also be found in the larger Greek dumps. Greece took a large batch of these after World War II ceased. These were originally shipped to England, in this case to help in the war effort in 1942 for the British Railways network. After the war they spread all over Europe, and can still be found in Turkey to this day.

Locomotive number 740-038, a 2-8-0 coal-burner. A freight-hauling engine seen here in Italy from Fortezza to San Candido – a real enthusiast's locomotive.

ITALY'S STEAM RAILWAY begun, as we have seen, by the Austro-Hungarian Empire, got underway once the country had achieved independence in 1861, and rapidly developed into an extensive system both north and south.

An example of Italy's greatest uses for steam in the latter years was in the dockland areas of Savona. Fourteen engines were purchased by a dock contractor named Emilio Estengo, whose company performed all the dock-shunting work. One of the most interesting engines run in this area of Italy was an 0-6-0 tank of the former Italian railways' 830 class. These tanks were formerly the shunting engines on the mainline Mediterranean railway, and were the forerunners of the better-known 835 class 0-6-0 shunting tanks which later became the standard shunting engines of the Italian railway system. These latter engines until recently existed in Italy on stand-by duty within dockland areas today, but there is little else outside museums of any merit for the enthusiast.

However, it is possible to witness Italian flavored steam today, as odd standby engines remain active, although many years have passed since freight and passenger work was steam traction. Much of the locomotion design then in use had been derived from the beginning of the century, standard class 740, a super-heated, 2-cylinder freight engine 2-8-0, of which a Franco Crosti boilered version was produced.

This masterpiece of Italian design was a gallant attempt to better utilize the hot gases from the fires, which had always been dissipated when it was ejected in the conventional method. Such ejection happened at a very high temperature, and heat loss resulted.

The modifications on the 740s fed the hot gases back from the smoke box through two large pre-heated drums containing the boiler-fed water. The gases were then exhausted at the fire box end, rather than at the chimney end as in other designs. The chimneys of these innovative engines were therefore placed at the rear of the engine. The method allowed the gases to exit the chimneys at a much lower temperature. The feed water was brought up to a high temperature in the pre-heated drums and fed into the

ITALY

At the station in Laurenzana, Italy, this 2-6-0 tank ran a now long defunct line.

A 2-6-2 passenger engine on the line from Fortezza to San Candido.

A 2-6-2 passenger express named "Regina."

A 2-8-0 freight engine on the Calalzo to Padua line in Italy.

(Opposite)
A freight-hauling 2-8-2 on the line from Trento to Venice. Seen here on the "Gocciadoro" viaduct.

(Right)
A passenger train 2-8-0 on a cold winter morning between Fortezza and San Candido.

boiler through a clack valve. Between 1941 and 1953 nearly one hundred engines were converted in this manner, and the saving was estimated to be about ten percent fuel. The initial incentive for the development was the British coal sanctions against Italy in the 30s. There is no indiginous coal in Italy, and the necessity of innovation produced this ingenious concept.

The system spread to other countries such as Spain, Belgium, and of course Britain where some of the last British service steam locomotives worked on the Crosti principle.

Engine 835 – an 0-6-0 shunting engine at Rovigo on the line to Chioggia.

Passenger locomotive No. 640 .003 — 2-6-0 coal burning steam on the line from Chivasso to Aosta.

Italian Railways 740 class 2-8-0
– the country's standard freight
design – during the last days of
steam traction in Italy.

One of the Italian State Railways magnificent high-wheeled 640 class 2-6-0, a type which brought a fine touch of vintage to latter-day steam operation.

IV

EASTERN EUROPE

An 0-4-4-0T Mallet · class 99, freight and passenger mixed service in East Germany between Gerode and Hergerode, one of the world-famous Mallets in green livery.

UNLESS, AS AN ENTHUSIAST, you have considerably more cash and can afford to visit India or China, Eastern Europe is probably one of the best hunting grounds for living steam locomotion.

In the next section we deal with Yugoslavia as a separate entity, because of the whole historical aspect of the breakup of the Austro-Hungarian Empire. Much of the Yugoslavian inheritance derived from this historical and political phenomenon was shared by other countries within the Eastern Bloc, as it is this area of the world – including Poland, Czechoslovakia and the other areas east of the Berlin Wall – which carried steam locomotion through into the present. Presumably steam still runs in the Iron Curtain countries because of the tight economic conditions and old-fashioned respect for the necessities of life. For the steam-locomotive enthusiast, this situation is entirely fortuitous, as it means that where possible much of the steam history can be exactly mapped

through exploratory visits across the communist borders.

The pictures in this chapter were all taken in recent years and have – like many other of the photographs in this book – never been seen before in publication.

The policy of most Eastern European countries today, in terms of transportation, appears to be to keep road economy to a minimum, and promote and improve railway transportation on an ongoing basis, continuing to use the steam facilities that are available. This can be witnessed throughout the cities and country areas by the fact that all the stations that a passenger will pass through still have their goods yards, and many steam locomotives are retained in good condition although lines are now rapidly going over to diesel and electric traction. This somewhat belies the western attitude that the Eastern Bloc European countries cannot afford to do "better." One might question exactly what is "better" about the crammed highways of the rest of Europe, the difficulties of private transport,

EAST GERMANY

(Opposite)
A working, East German 2-10-2T between Nordhausen and Wernigerode.

(Right)
Locomotive number 50-3553, a 2-10-0 freight engine, but in this case hauling passenger coaches to Quedlinburg in East Germany.

and the railway services that are not necessarily any more efficient than the still-running steam locomotive railways.

Certainly the attitudes of railway authorities or state authorities of Russia, Prussia and Austria, before the First World War, have been carried through into Polish workmanship, engineering and the running of the PKP lines ("Polski Koleje Panstwowe" – Polish National Railway), which not only ferry their passengers on time from city to city, but also provide even a tourist interest to those who wish to come and sample what the Poles have made of their inherited railway traditions.

Locomotives are specially prepared for carrying tourists and children on holiday trips, for example to the Wenecja Railway Museum and the historic Slavonic Fort at Bishkupin. Both these sites are tremendous tourist attractions, and visitors come by main line train to Znin before taking the branch line to the museum and fort. The line is run by the state railway, and although freight traffic is run on the line, special coaches are bedecked with designs and devices for children from school-parties. Within this narrow-gauge Wenecja Railway Museum there are, of course, many delights for the steam

(This page)
A 2-6-2T hauling passenger train between Hasselfelde and Nordhausen.

(Opposite)
A class 41 mixed-traffic 2-8-2, one of the standard designs conceived during the 1920s after the unification of Germany.

(Opposite)
Another German 41 class 2-8-2 mixed traffic.

(Right)
Locomotive 99-5904 - 0-4-4-0T Mallet, freight and passenger.

enthusiast. One example is a TX2 class 0-8-0 tank which was the forerunner of the famous Feldbahns, mentioned previously.

Out on the much-used tracks of Poland there is another prime example of great locomotion: the Polish State Railways TKT 48 class 2-8-2T. One likely location to find such engines is the depot at Klodzko in Silesia, southern Poland, close to the Czechoslovakian border. The TKT 48s are a superb middle-range engine for secondary lines or fast-moving suburban branch operation. One hundred were built by Chrzanow, and ninety-four more by Cegielski – both Polish builders – and amongst their duties had been the hauling of Warsaw's last suburban service. Polish engine builders gained a great reputation from their work on these locomotives.

A number of these engines survive on the Klodzko service running to Kudowa Zdroj. Many of the through-trains from this town to Wroclaw begin their journey to Klodzko behind the TKT 48s, after which one of the superb PT47 class 2-8-2 "Mikados" takes the train forward to Wroclaw.

The PT47 is probably one of the most epic locomotives left in European service. Of all the engines on Polish railways, these are the most perfect exam-

(Opposite)
A TX class 0-8-0T – the very last survivor – on the line from Znin to Gasaw, in rural Poland.

(Below)
The coat-of-arms of the Polish State Railways which appears on almost all Polish steam traction – PKP stands for Polski Koleje Panstwowe.

ples of the Polish school of design. Enthusiasts visiting Poland should not miss the chance to view these wonderful engines, so long as they survive.

As mentioned earlier, the Polish designs are descended to a large extent from other influences, including German, but many refinements and additions were made by the Polish State Railways themselves – a kind of beautifying of German esthetics. All these engines were built between the end of the 1940s and the beginning of the 1950s, sixty of them by Cegielski of Poznan, and one hundred and twenty by Chzranow.

The PT47 has all the characteristics of a Pacific in that they are extremely fast engines but, as the Mikados, they orient towards moderate speeds with heavier trains and more rapid starts. Nevertheless their running speed is a regular sixty miles per hour.

These locomotives have, in recent months, at the time of writing, received

POLAND

their last complete overhaul, and probably within the next two years they will be phased out altogether.

As a tribute to the continuing Polish railway services, it is worth quoting a diary entry made when visiting Poland and watching the Karkonosze Express passing through Bardo Slaskie Station to the north of Klodzko. "My pulse quickened as the clock inched its way up to 22.50, the time the express was scheduled to pass. The silence served to increase the tension till, on the second, the color light flicked to green. The tremors that followed transformed the atmosphere; the platform shook in a manner such as had frightened me as a child, as with a tremendous roar, the Karkonosze burst from the tunnel. The vivid glow from the cab made rippling orange patterns in the smoke, and the station lights momentarily lit the huge, spinning, driving wheels. The station became enveloped in the scent of hot oil and smoke soon to be wafted away by the speeding coaches and sleeping-cars. With speeds in the sixties, the tail lights quickly receded, matched by the color signal as it returned to red. The mighty magician had passed, and I

(Opposite and right)
Studies of Polish State Railways' TKT 48 class 2-8-2Ts amidst smoky blue of the depot at Klodzko in Silesia, Poland, close to the Czech border. TKTs are middle range mixed-traffic engines, in widespread use in Poland.

was back in the real age of steam once more – for what I had witnessed was not a fantasy. The crisp exhausts of the PT47 receded through the clear damp night. The moths danced around the dim platform light, and once again the rain began to fall."

A typical polish steam scene of today depicting three former German Kriegslokomotivs 2-10-0s.

Inside the narrow gauge railway museum at Wenecja. On the left is a TX26 class 0-8-0 tank. On the right, a TX 2 0-8-0 tank of German industrial origin and built in 1911 – this latter being the forerunner of the German military Feldbahn engines of the First World War.

A Hungarian classic engine
working on the Jesenice to Nova
Gorica line in Slovenia – an
engine that was ceded to
Yugoslavia when the Austro-
Hungarian Empire broke up
after the First World War.

THE FIRST WORLD WAR was of great significance, not only for its renowned destruction of life, but also for the effect it had on territorial boundaries. Yugoslavia is a good example of what happened once the war was over. Prior to 1914 in the area which is now clearly defined as Yugoslavia, there were countries with other names. There was Croatia, Slovania, parts of the Austro-Hungarian Empire – almost totally differently defined in terms of their boundaries, and so naturally in terms of the railway lines they had developed.

The formation of Yugoslavia after the First World War included locomotives from the former Hungarian territories, that is, Croatia, the old Austrian area of Slovenia, along with Serbia and Bosnia which were formerly under Ottoman rule.

We see, on opening this chapter, an example of this inheritance. A Hungarian classic on the Jesenice-to-Nova-Gorica line in Slovenia in 1972. The example here is a 2-6-2 branch line tank engine. This type was originally the

YUGOSLAVIA

Hungarian Railways' 342 class, introduced in 1915 to supercede the smaller 375 class. By 1918 three hundred of these locomotives were in traffic on suburban duties around Budapest and widespread branch line work across the Austro-Hungarian territories. Such engines were powerful and effective enough to enhance any empire's strength.

When Yugoslavia took over Croatia and Slovenia from the Empire, it received eighty-six of the engines of this type, and then a further two engines of the same type after World War II reparations were granted.

On these pages you can see another example of prime locomotive beauty at work in Yugoslavia. The engine runs for the Yugoslavian State Railway and is an 06 class 2-8-2 steaming in this picture across the railway bridge at Maribor in Slovenia with a stopping train from Cacovec.

The 06s are significant in Yugoslavian railway development in that they were one of three standard designs introduced in 1930 – the 05 "Pacific" for fast passenger work, the 06 Mikado for mixed traffic duties, and the 30

class 2-10-0 for heavy freight. These standard designs were built in fact for the railways of the Kingdom of Serbs, Croats and Slovenes. There were thirty 06 engines, all built by Borsig of Berlin in 1930.

Traveling in Yugoslavia the enthusiast may enjoy some memorable scenes, for example on the river bridge at Maribor in Slovenia: perhaps looking across it on an early summer morning as the sun is just rising and the morning mists disperse, one might see a classic of Yugoslavian locomotive history, a class 25 2-8-0 of the Yugoslavian State Railway, originally an Austrian engine ceded to Yugoslavia when the Austro-Hungarian Empire was sliced up. The 25 class engines are descended from an Austrian design originally built by the legendary chief mechanical engineer, Karl Golsdorf, and date back to 1897 to the Austrian 170 class two-cylinder compound 2-8-0. The 170s were two cylinder according to the Golsdorf policy, and after his death a "superheated" simple version of the 170 was produced and classified as Austrian 270. These are the engines which now make up the Yugoslavian 25 class. Altogether a total of fourteen hundred – some 170s and some 270s – were built, and some of those that came to Yugoslavia were delivered new.

Another classic Yugoslavian design is the 51 class engine depicted on page 150 – an inherited Hungarian tank engine – a 2-6-2, originally Hungarian 375 class, introduced onto the Hungarian railways in 1907 for light branch and connecting lines, of which there were many during the Empire days.

This engine weighed fifty-four tons, with only an eleven-ton axle-loading, making them perfect for light work. The construction of these particular engines went on right up until 1959 – fifty years of building life. Ninety-eight of these 375s passed to Croatia from the Austro-Hungarian Empire. In 1929 thirty more were ordered new by Yugoslavia for the Maschinenabrik in Budapest, with a further fifty engines built in Yugoslavia itself at Slavonski Brod. Finally, another twenty came to the country as part of a reparation package after World War II. The most extraordinary thing about these 51 class locomotives is their antiquated appearance: they hardly look as though they could have been constructed as recently as the 1950s for a European country.

Yugoslavia, though, retains its steam in the same fashion as East Germany, largely because it appreciates the workhorse capacity of locomotives that

(Opposite)
A scene on the Karlovac to Sisak line in Croatia. The engine is a 51 class 2-6-2.

(Right)
A scene in Slovenia – showing a Prussian G12 3-cylinder 2-10-0, a magestic veteran of the Yugoslav Railway network.

have been functioning without rest for so many years. In any event, the economic restrictions of the country prevent the rapid growth of diesel which means that steam is cared for and kept in good condition. It cannot be called in any way "glamorous," however, for the locomotives are generally black and functioning under industrial conditions. Nevertheless this small, growing Eastern European nation, with one foot in the West, has the great pleasure of enthusiasts the world over, isolated pockets of veteran locomotives which befit the country's rich railway heritage.

V

MIDDLE EAST

This engine was built for the old Baghdad Railway in 1911 and now serves on Turkey's Black Sea coast in tripping work for a local factory, carrying clay.

TURKISH STEAM has diminished over the last fifteen years, but – as will be known by almost anyone interested in steam loco-motion – it is still in evidence in a large area of industry. Karabuk, in the mountains of northern Turkey, south of the Black Sea coast, is the scene of one of the country's largest steel industries, set high in the mountains deliberately to prevent easy air attack. Classic types used in these steelworks are the 0-6-0 "Sad-dle Tank," built in Newcastle, England, by Robert Stephenson and Hawthorn. The name of the steelworks is "Ulke," and it lies on the railway line from Zonguldak on the Black Sea coast. The works were actually the very first steel plant in Turkey, and ordained by Kemel Ataturk himself.

Six 0-6-0 Saddle Tanks work this region, two of them built by the British manufacturers especially for the industrial complex when it opened in that year. The rest were delivered during and after World War II. So far as the author is aware, at least at the time of writing, these particular engines still survive today.

The saddle tanks of these engines hold one thousand gallons of water – the engines in working order weigh forty-one and a half tons, with a tractive effort of 22,118 pounds.

Turkey, as we know, is divided clean in half – one side in the European sector, and the other effectively part of the "Orient." In the European sector there is little steam, but beyond the Bosphorous there are many place where enthusiasts will reap rewards. There are a few restric-tions on photography, but the Turkish people welcome tourists to their country.

One of the major influences that still exist today derived from the mighty and disastrous Third Reich, as well as the Bismark administration before that in Germany. It is appropriate that in Turkey the engines most needed are heavy and powerful, with tremendous pulling power, and these type of locomotive have come directly from the battlefields of Germany. One of the types that the German army relied heavily upon for their weapon hauling and troop movements was the "Kriegslocomotive," a type that survived some pretty incredible conditions,

TURKEY

Fiering a main line steam locomotive insured physical fitness
as often several tons of coal
would be manually shovelled
into the firebox.

On the colliery system at Cata-lagi with a standard gauge 0-6-0T built by Henschel in 1918 on the left alongside a meter gauge tank built by Bagnals in England in 1942.

(This page)
An 0-10-0 – ex-Prussian G10 –
shot on the Afyon to Dinar line
in Turkey and (opposite) a 4-8-0
Henschel, built in Germany, on
the Mersin to Adana line, also
in Turkey.

(Opposite)
Double-headed 2-10-0s leaving the yard at Irmak. Eighty-eight of these were built at the Vulcan Ironworks in Pennsylvania and exported to Turkey.

(Right)
Another example of Prussian design, this one in the form of the G8^2 2-8-0, a smaller descendent of the G12 2-10-0s.

often punished continuously throughout the war effort. Six thousand of this particular engine were built before, during and after World War II, and some still exist in Turkey. No modern diesel engine would ever have survived such workloads as the war produced, let alone go on working in almost parallel conditions for forty years thereafter. Also on the Black Sea coast at a place called Eregli, it is still possible to find Prussian-designed locomotives of the class G82 2-8-0s on a fascinating little network of Turkish railways, isolated from the rest of the Turkish railway system. This small railway runs from the Armutcuk Colliery down to Eregli Docks, where the coal is put on board ship. The line is only seventeen kilometers long, and the engines are maintained at the Eregli works except when serious maintenance work is needed, in which case the locomotives themselves are craned on board the ships and taken away to larger works, while another of the same type is brought in to replace them.

The line travels by the Black Sea coast itself, along gradients as sharp as one-in-forty.

As mentioned, these G82s belong to a celebrated family of Prussian freight

Many secondary line passenger trains in Turkey are still hauled by former German war engines – 2-10-0s often maintained in resplendent condition.

A typical Turkish branch-line scene with one of the world's last ex-Prussian G8 0-8-0s.

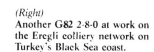
(Right)
Another **G82** 2-8-0 at work on the Eregli colliery network on Turkey's Black Sea coast.

engines, forming in a way a smaller version of the Prussian G12s. Over one thousand were made, sixty-two of which were built specially for Turkey between 1927 and 1935, long after Prussia had disappeared as a country altogether. The builders were Nohab and Tubize.

The G82 lacked that certain Teutonic precision which is so characteristic of most of the engines that came from Prussia. In order to implement the reduction of the G82 from its originally-designed size, wheels were removed, the boiler, fire box and tubes therefore shortened accordingly – all perfectly efficient except that the tubes were left at the same diameter with a shorter boiler, causing the gases to enter the fire box at too high a temperature. The G82 suffered for this defect, but in every other respect they are a magnificent example of Prussian design.

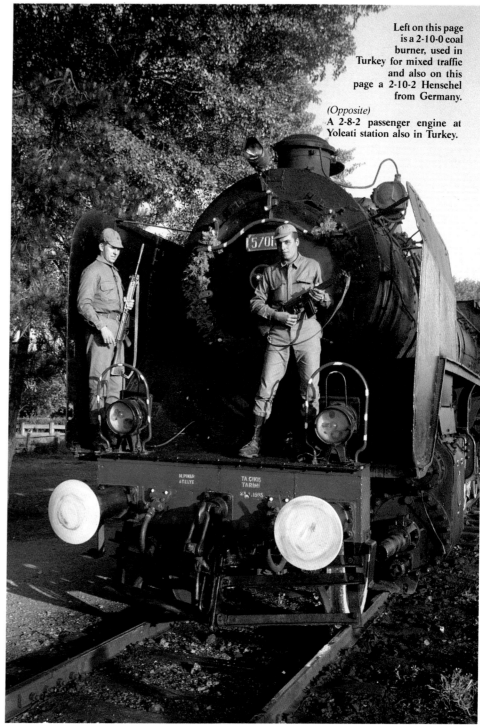

Left on this page is a 2-10-0 coal burner, used in Turkey for mixed traffic and also on this page a 2-10-2 Henschel from Germany.

(Opposite)
A 2-8-2 passenger engine at Yolcati station also in Turkey.

(Opposite)
**A Turkish State Railways
2-8-0 shunting the colliery yard
at Armuteuk.**

(Right)
**Oiling up on a Turkish freight
engine.**

For many years the Turkish State Railways have tried to phase out their steam traction in favor of dieselization. But this plan has yet to come to fruition, and in 1987 when all steam locomotives should have been phased out, engines were actually being re-instated from condemned dumps. This was because of unreliability with diesel traction and the constant shortage of the complex spare parts needed. Today it is therefore still possible to see and enjoy examples of famous locomotive types which have made Turkey a great attraction and are extinct elsewhere. Types such as: XLMS Stanier 8F 2-8-0s, German war engines, Prussian G8s and G10s, Robert Stephenson's 2-8-2s and German 4-8-0s of classic styling.

How long this wonderful situation will continue, no one knows, but it does emphasize the tremendous longevity of steam traction once a will exists to maintain it.

Engines are also well maintained east of the Bosphorous where engineer's yards take on the work where possible, or the broken engines are shipped away for heavier repair. Visiting Turkey is something of an unexpected treat as the people are often willing to welcome tourists with cameras and there

(Opposite)
An 0-8-0 German built, originally Prussian designed locomotive, delivered to Turkey in 1924.

(Right)
A 2-10-0 built slightly later in 1948 in America.

are usually few problems about going to most parts and taking shots of the engines at work. Of all the European countries, Turkey is the most favored by enthusiasts, especially as few restrictions exist on railway photography compared with the steam-operating states of the Eastern bloc.

(Opposite)
An industrial steam locomotive in one of its traditional guises - hauling molten metal waste.

(This page)
A Turkish State Railways **G82** 2-8-0 trundles across the metals of the Eregli colliery system.

VI

AFRICA

Sennar Junction, close to the Ethiopian border, probably the best center for steam in Sudan. The engines visible are, right, 310 class Mikado from northern England in 1952 and, left, passenger-hauling 220 class 4-6-2 Pacifics built in the 1940s.

STEAM LOCOMOTION is considered sufficiently vital in the third world to have warranted attention from a western fund-raising drive. In 1986 six boilers from 310 class Mikado engines and 220 class Pacifics were shipped to England to the Hugh Phillips works in South Wales for major overhaul work under the Band-Aid program set up by Bob Geldof to raise money for Ethiopian and Sudanese famine. A batch of these 310 engines run from Sennar Junction to Damazeen on the Ethiopian border, handling light traffic in the Sudan. Heavier traffic in the country is handled by 500 class 4-8-2s, 42 of which were delivered from the North British works in Glasgow in 1955. By the early 1980s only two of these remained. Derelict examples lie around the system, specially at Atbara works where many await spares.

Third World countries have certain requirements that do not exist elsewhere, and steam locomotion suits those requirements to a large extent.

SUDAN

Many of their railway systems operate mixed trains – a combination of freight and passenger within one train! This might not suit the western commuter very much, but in parts of Africa it is not unusual to see an engine shunting at all the wayside stations, picking up products, and setting down merchandise and passengers alike along the way. Imagine a diesel locomotive traveling from New York to Chicago stopping en route to shunt freight, pick up elephant dung, and drop off fifty head of cattle before arriving in the passenger station!

In developing countries also, the roads are hardly sophisticated enough to carry any major motor vehicle traffic. With the shortage of cars the railway system is even more of a lifeline. Africa could have been advancing through the beginnings of an industrial revolution, with communications and industry growing up around the steam locomotive, were it not for a major decrease in progress in those parts no longer controlled by the "white man." Sadly, even the steam trains are barely being used to their full potential.

One of the Sudan Railways' North-British-built Mikado 2-8-2s heads along the lightly laid branch from Sennar to Damazeen.

Of course, as any railway enthusiast will know, the conquering of African terrain by railway was pioneered by Cecil Rhodes, the greatest of Africa's early railway pioneers. His task was to get the diamonds from the south to the seaboard and then, once he had accomplished this major task, to drive north through the entire African plain. He was heavily discouraged by competitive Dutch landowners in the Transvaal but this opposition did little but drive him harder and faster.

One of the most extraordinary stories is in relation to his determination to cross the great Victoria Falls. The Falls could not be a tougher natural boundary to cross, if only for their width and the hardness of the rock, but not satisfied with having the line built from one side to the other, Rhodes was absolutely set on having the trains pass close enough to the massive rapids to have the water splash on the windows of the carriages! Additionally there was no way of approaching the job of laying the track except from the way he was coming, from the south, so that the equipment for building the bridge and the track on the other side had to be taken over on a suspended wire. The wire was hitched up, strong enough to carry ten-ton weights and everything that was needed simply swung across the Falls. The railway line on the other side of the water could therefore be continued even while the bridge across was still under construction! Rhodes himself did not live to see the Falls bridged, but died two years before the first magnificent engine pulled passenger coaches across.

His spirit built the African railway system – as so often in railway pioneering, it was the strength and stubborn determination of one man that got things done.

A 4-8-0 tender engine, originally built as a 4-10-2T. The removal of the tanks reduces adhesion so that the splashers are filled with scrap iron to make up the loss.

THE SITUATION in many of Africa's developing nations is not at all simple. There are locomotives, and they still form the only available railway transport system; but very often, as in Ghana, they cannot be run.

The Ghana railway is presently almost at a complete standstill. The railway system there is run by Indian officials who have forbidden the use of steam on ideological grounds!

Diesel is difficult to maintain and many railwaymen prefer the simplicity of steam.

Gangs of volunteers are therefore struggling to get some sort of railway system working so that the heavy commodities available in Ghana can be exported to bolster the flagging foreign-exchange requirements.

The British built the first main-line of the Gold Coast from Sekondi inland through the inhospitable, malaria-infested jungles, starting the building in 1899 and they reached Kumasi in 1905. The original motion was to pioneer the Gold Coast's gold reserves, which lay behind the dense belt of jungle in-

GHANA

land. Still there today is the period British Sekondi station, which was moved to a deeper water port at Takoradi in 1920, with the superb rolling stock lying abandoned around the yards and the Gents clock from Leicester still on the station wall – long since stopped. The Ghanians have been considering situating a railway museum at the old station to commemerate Ghana's rich railway history, while work still goes on in an attempt to get the railway itself on its feet again. Every nut and bolt of the Gold Coast railway was British supplied, and when the Gold Coast became independent from England, the country was tipped to be one of the richest and most successful of the African states, with its relatively sophisticated population, good industries and first class railway. But within a decade a tragic decline set in which affected the railway. There were political malpractices which bankrupted the economy which in turn ran down the railway so it could no longer shift the heavy commodities for export. Today the Ghanians fight to retain their railway, and many Ghanian railwaymen would like to see British personnel amongst them once more.

The South African railway system was born out of the discovery of diamonds, the determination of one man – Cecil Rhodes – and a pioneering spirit that braved lions, rapids and vast terrain.

THE RICHES AND ENERGY of South Africa present a totally different picture from that in Ghana. During the 1970s, and still to a great extent today, one of the busiest steam railway lines runs through South Africa. For nine miles north of Bloemfontein on the mainline to Kroonstad, trains climb through nine miles of one-in-a-hundred gradients and standing on a hillside on busy days, one could see steam from four separate trains at one time. Sadly this route is now electrified.

SOUTH AFRICA

This line was worked entirely by South African 4-8-2s: the 15F class introduced in 1938 and the larger 23 class engines. And it was normal to see double-headed freight trains climbing northwards through the South African veldt. One of these engines could take one thousand, two hundred and fifty tons over the route, and two together could handle two thousand tons.

Another great and fascinating engine that until recently ran in this troubled country takes the line from De Arr to Beaufort West through the arid Karroo desert. It is the huge condenser, 25 class 4-8-4, one of the last condensing engines to run in world service. Before these engines were introduced, water had to be carried into the Karroo desert and tanks filled to replenish the locomotives that passed through. The class 25s were built by North British of Glasgow and made it possible to get through the desert without watering. The principle was that once the steam had driven the pistons, instead of being exhausted from the chimney it was passed back to the tender where it went through condenser elements to be turned back into warm water again, whereupon it would be pumped back into the boiler. This recycling process enabled the condensers to run for seven hundred miles without replenishing a drop of water. In order to "pull" on the fire – a task done in other engines by the exhausted steam from the chimney – a steam-driven fan was placed in the engine's smoke-box to create the necessary draft.

(This page)
One of the many vintage British-built industrial locomotives surviving in South Africa.

(Opposite)
Steam operations in South Africa are some of the most exciting on earth, as this scene of a Garratt heading northwards from Cape Town proves.

(This page)
A surviving member of the class 8, South African 4-8-0 originally built for main line service but since pensioned off into industrial usage.

(Opposite and right)
A huge condenser 25 class 4-8-4 working the line between De Arr and Beaufort West through the arid Karroo desert – these were the very last condensers engines to run – the condensers provided a recycling of the steam back through the condenser and into the boiler once more. These engines could cover seven hundred miles without watering.

These locomotives ran through the Karroo desert well into the late 1970s with both freight and passenger trains. The most recognizable element was the long tender which actually almost equalled the locomotive in size because of the condensing elements.

The journey was one hundred and sixty-four miles from De Arr to Beaufort West, and the engine had a grate area of seventy square feet with a tractive effort of 51,410 pounds. Sadly, the very ingenuity of the condensers brought the engines out of service before they would have otherwise been without such complex devices. The condensers themselves were far too difficult to maintain, and something simpler was sought to replace them.

One of the interesting practices of the South African railway engineers is to hybridize their engines by making tender engines out of tank engines. The result of this is a reduction in adhesion when the tank is removed on the main driving wheel. Without good adhesion, the shifting of heavy coal trains becomes difficult. In order to make up for the lack, large "splashers" are mounted and filled with scrap iron or concrete.

A scene from one of the British Empire-built railways – from Mombasa along the Indian Ocean climbing inland to Nairobi – 332 miles. Mountain class Garratts hauled 1,200 ton loads and weighed, in themselves, at 252 tons.

KENYA HAS ONE OF THE MOST remarkable railways in the world. The photograph on the left was taken on the line from Mombasa, on the Indian Ocean, that climbs the steep coastal escarpment inland to Nairobi, Kenya's capital, three hundred and thirty-two miles inland.

The line at this time was worked by two-hundred-and-fifty-two-ton Mountain class Garratts pulling up the sharp incline out of Mombasa through the heart of the green coastal belt. Within this coastal belt, the high rainfall levels produced a beautiful green hue to the land. But when the line reaches some one hundred miles inland, the rain reduces dramatically, and the landscape becomes golden scrub and stunted bush, looking more like a game reserve.

These Mountain class Garratts were permitted to take twelve hundred tons over the lines on the single track route, which includes gradients of one-in-sixty. The journey can take as long as twenty-five hours, and the crew have three shifts with sleeping cabooses within the train.

Historically, Kenya saw its first railway efforts in 1896 when the rail was laid at Mombasa. Five years later in 1901, the first train ran from Mombasa to Kisumu on the shores of Lake Victoria, linking the Indian Ocean with Lake Victoria. The total cost of the railway at that time was five million UK pounds.

The Mombasa line was probably the busiest in East Africa, laid with ninety-five-pound rails to accomodate twenty-one-ton axle-loadings of the Garratts. The haulage tonnage was so great, and the terrain so rough, that East African railways contemplated a three-hundred-and-seventy-two-ton 4-8-4, plus 4-8-4 Garratt, with a twenty-six-ton axle-loading – almost half as big again as the 59s, but the engine was never built. This sad loss was partly because the smaller running engine was so successful, but also because of East Africa's awareness of the potential of diesel traction. The heaviest engine would have been a 61 class. But only diesel runs today. However, at the time of writing persistent rumors exist that some of the big Mountain class Garratts are being put back into service.

KENYA

BANYARUANDA

A 31 class 2-8-2 "Tribal" engine seen under repair at Tabora – especially built for the East African Railways which included Kenya, Tanzania and Uganda.

OTH THE ENGINES DEPICTED in this section belong to the "Tribal" class, specially built for the East African Railways Corporation which covered Kenya, Tanzania and Uganda. Sadly, this corporation no longer exists.

These two engines are from a very interesting family of locomotives. The one on this spread is a 31 class 2-8-4 Tribal, number 3116 Banyaivanda, here seen under repair at Tabora. The picture on the page of the next spread was taken at Voi, and is engine number 3128 Japadhola on the connecting line from Mombasa to Nairobi mainline. Voi is the junction that connects the main-line into Tanzania from Kenya.

The Tribals consist of three types: the 29 class 2-8-2, the 30 class 2-8-4, and the 31 class 2-8-4. These Tribals derived originally from Nigerian Railways 2-8-2 River class, which are similar in appearance, and form the backbone of East African steam power, some still remaining in service today. The 29s have a heavier axle-loading than the 30s or 31s, which are able to take

into account the lightly laid tracks of East Africa. They are highly standardized with interchangeable parts, all named, with Gisel chimneys and rectangular brass name-plates, as can be seen in the picture on this page.

The naming of steam locomotives was once a tradition practiced in many parts of the world – the name invariably being noble and evocative – but this attitude to steam locomotives has long gone.

The 29 class came from the North British of Glasgow in 1951-55 when thirty-one were built, the 30 class between 1955-56, and the 31 class in the same years from the Vulcan Foundry in Lancashire.

The many political changes that have erupted in the African continent have not helped to speed up the advance of railways all over this vast and sometimes primitive land. African conditions require great energy for industrial growth and also for the demands of the people who, like Indians, have an incredible love of travel. The experience of sampling the railway in Africa is extraordinary as you can find yourself either in relatively luxurious conditions – i.e. at least on a seat of some kind – or uncom-

TANZANIA

A scene on the East African Railways, taken at Voi – engine number 3128 "Jopadhola" on the connecting line from Mombasa to Nairobi.

fortably jammed between two large African ladies on a wooden bench. People travel cheek by jowl with animals on their way to the market and it is not at all unusual for an engine to uncouple its load in order to go off and do some other work for a few hours, while the passengers remain encased on a railway siding, patiently, or sometimes not so patiently, waiting for their carrier to return.

The overpowering smells, the dirty conditions, the incredible amount of noise and not to mention conditions which are invariably overcrowded, might not appeal to the average European traveler accustomed to British Rail or the luxury and speed of most railway systems elsewhere in the world, but as a single experience it is certainly one that will be remembered to tell to your grandchildren!

In addition, of course, the African terrain, almost everywhere you go, is so dramatic that it is probable that new travelers to this continent will hardly notice what is going on inside the carriage as they gaze out at a land which takes the breath away with its primitive and natural conditions.

Frequently the animal life will come very close to the passing trains; the trains have become an accustomed sight to lions and most of the other wild creatures that live right next to the tracks. Engines have been known to come to a complete standstill in order for an entire lion family to cross the track safely.

A pair of Beyer-Peacock-built 14A class 2-6-2 + 2-6-2 Garratts storming through typical African terrain on the line from West Nicholson to Bulawayo, photographed in the early 1970s.

ZIMBABWE

ON LINE FROM WEST NICHOLSON to Bulawayo during the early 1970s when Zimbabwe was Rhodesia, the picture on the left shows a Beyer Peacock built 14A class 2-6-2, plus a 2-6-2 Garratt storming through typical African terrain. Since this picture was taken there have been some changes with regard to steam locomotion; but all the locomotives are still Garratts, and the two engines shown here still receive heavy overhauls between their long bouts of strenuous work.

The Garratt engines helped the colonization of Africa, in the same way as its articulated relation, the Mallet engines colonized America. The Garratt locomotive was designed and patented by H.W. Garratt in 1907, and Beyer Peacock of Manchester in England took up the building with caution. Garratt sadly died young – at forty-nine years of age in 1913 – but did see the first fruits of his design as they were exported from England. However, he failed to live long enough to witness the effect his work had throughout much of the world.

The engines were ideally built for heavy-freight haulage and passenger duties on rough lines, and so saw great success in many part of Africa, and almost totally dominate Zimbabwe's steam services today.

There is nothing in Africa so dramatic as the sight depicted on the opposite page – the indomitable double-header Garratt pulling heavy freight of over a thousand tons. The double-headers will always have a wagon between the two Garratts to spread the weight on the track. Within this mighty continent one legend that has recently become of romantic interest to the world is that of Karen Blixen, the Danish author who spent much of her life in Africa. A pioneering woman whose home was on the barren plains of some of the wildest parts of the continent, Karen Blixen wrote most of what is now best-selling literature while managing a coffee plantation! *Out of Africa* was a movie of hers set in this glorious land when steam locomotion was at its peak throughout the world; it was she who predicted that the locomotive would create the final schism between the black man and the white. The flowering of a

(Opposite)
Former Rhodesian Railways 14A class 2-6-2 + 2-6-2 Garratt number 516 takes refreshment at Balla Balla on the West Nicholson-to-Bulawayo line.

(Right)
A class 12 4-8-2 built in Britain between 1926 and 1930 still running in Zimbabwe, having been delivered originally to Rhodesia before independence from the British Empire.

primitive nation can often be the death of the old race, perhaps one that has occupied the land for centuries, as was the case in Zimbabwe. Africa today struggles against the advancements of the rest of the world, suffering from some of the most serious droughts in history and the most terrible starvation problems – such as publicized when Ethiopia hit the headlines. Alongside such natural disasters comes political chaos, a consequence of national growth which was especially evident during the steam engine's zenith and which has made considerable contributions to its decline. In fact political upheaval has not contributed merely to the decline of steam but to that of railways per se – in certain section of Africa at least. What steam remains today is still very hard-worked. Any change to diesel must either be a gradual one or a development which entails tremendous cost. Africa could therefore be one part of the world where steam continues into the twenty-first century, if the African countries settle their internal troubles.

VII
PACIFIC ISLANDS

The 3ft 6in gauge main line network on Java is the Madiun locomotive graveyard with two giant Mallet engines that once worked the little island.

THE PICTURE ON THE left of this spread is a graveyard scene from the Madiun locomotive works on the three-foot, six-inch mainline network of Java. The two giant Mallet engines once worked over the island's volcanic highlands.

The engine on the right is an Indonesian State Railways' class DD51, an original American-built Alco 2-8-8-0 four-cylinder Mallet, of 1919. This engine is a scaled-down replica of a type that worked over the North American prairies in the early twentieth century. Though scaled-down these engines had super power on the smaller gauge network of the developing countries.

The DD52 (left) was of European origin from Hartmann of Germany, built in 1924 with its low-pressure cylinder fully in evidence. In the foreground of this picture, in the left hand corner, can be seen the scrap remains of number DD5106. It related to the engine behind it – the works' plate still visible on the right side – Richard Hartmann of Chemnitz. Also one can see

INDONESIA

the lamp from a B53 class 4-4-0, plus broken parts of a locomotive wheel, and pieces of flanged piping, all lying like the guts of an animal! Before very long the jungle will cover the whole graveyard.

Over the page on the right of the next spread can be seen a B51 class 4-4-0 express passenger engine. Thirty-nine of these were built for the Dutch East Indies, as Java was once called, between 1900 and 1909. The builders were largely German – Hanomag and Hartmann – though a few of the engines were Dutch built, from Werkspoor of Amsterdam.

This type was the main and most important express passenger locomotive on Java, and in appearance is of nineteenth century Prussian-built ancestry. They are esthetically beautiful, with a low-slung boiler, tall, elegant chimney and huge domes and splashers. On the engine's left side, the low-pressure cylinder is five hundred and eighty millimeters in diameter.

Sadly these locomotives have long since been replaced in the main line duty, and work their very last days on stopping trains between Tanahabang

(Opposite)
A veteran 2-4-0 passenger engine built by Sharp Stewart of Manchester during the 1880s heads gingerly along the branch from Madiun to Ponorogo in Java.

(Right)
Indonesian State Railways B51 class 4-4-0 on shed at Rangkasbitung in 1974.

– a suburb of Jakarta – up to Rangkasbitung, forty-five miles to the west.

Java's steam railway was like a working museum until the end of the 1970s, but now sadly the majority of the antiquities have gone.

But many of the best photographic material that exists in archives such as the author's come from this part of the world, where engines have worked their last days in conditions of extreme hardship.

"Puffing Billy" in Australia.

THE FIRST RAILWAY TO MAKE its way across Australia was in the small colonized area called New South Wales – a British colony and therefore, naturally, it did so with British locomotives and expertise. The first engines were ordered in 1853 for the pioneer Sydney and Paramatta Railway, which was part of the Australian determination to bridge Sydney and the Western plains, between which lay the legendary Blue Mountains. Some twenty-five miles from the coast of New South Wales is this solid wall of mountains, extending endlessly in both directions and up four thousand feet! The pioneers had two alternatives to go, and this illustrates the energy that went into steam railway in those days. They could either surmount gradients of one-in-twenty and go over the mountains, or they could tunnel two miles through them. Local engineers were nervous, at the least, about tunneling this distance in such primitive conditions, and, in any case, ten million bricks were needed to make the tunnel wall, and no one at the time had the slightest idea how they were ever

AUSTRALIA

going to get ten million bricks to the site! The decision was to zig zag over the mountains in a similar way to the method used in the Ghats Mountains in India. The Lithgow Zig Zag in Australia still exists today, though there have been some new alignments for railway travel, and the original and very beautiful alignment is only visible from a road in the midst of thick forest.

Conquering the lands of Australia with railway track was a truly unique experience. Unlike in Africa, there were no lions to eat the workers; and unlike in America, there were no Indians to scalp them or vast rivers to scale, and further into the center of the continent there were no mountains to be tunneled. In fact there was literally nothing at all – not a single thing to surmount except the blazing and scalding sun of Central Australia.

The work gangs had to take everything with them, food, equipment, and of course, water – especially water. Camels were taken as draught animals, and the service stations that were set up along the way became the homes,

Engine 3026, a Beyer Peacock
4-6-0 Mount Victoria.

and then the towns, of the men who built the railway, and the places where all the railway maintenance eventually happened.

Once again the steam railway was responsible for creating a nation.

There is a particular flavor in Australia that has always stood by the harder-working aspects of life, and the building of the railway there brought great stories of adventure amongst the workers and engineers, a few of which still survive amongst the older men. As in other parts of the world, particularly England, there are men in their seventies, eighties and nineties who remember the legends.

One such was found near Sydney who recalled the times when the "Trans" was still being run with steam. He tells the story of the Kangaroos that lived on the "outback" plains where lines were still fresh to the area. Because of the long distances and the frequent watering places that were needed to keep the engines running, and because of the kangaroos' tendency to friendliness with the people, the animals frequently moved their places of habitat to these areas. The more remote watering stations were manned by a few, often small, families who began to build what would later develop into towns, and during there early days the kangaroos were sometimes part of the family – after a fashion! This particular story tells of an engine tender that had been left in the watering area for repair for some weeks while parts were brought in from Sydney by a crew of repair men. The family tending the watering center had left for a while for food and supplies and returned to find that the kangaroos' whole family had made the tender their own personal home. Getting them to leave was more of task than had been anticipated and in the end the tender had to be replaced by a specially built shack which the family erected so that the tender could go back into service! A case of nature making the best of mechanics.

A brace of fine steam survivors on the Hawaiian-Philippine network. On the left is a 0-6-2ST and on the right an 0-6-0, both built by Baldwins, USA.

PHILIPPINES

THE PHILIPPINE ISLANDS have to be a visiting place for the enthusiast, for here, there are fine sights for the romantically inclined locomotive lover. A fine stable of decrepit American veterans scaled down to three-foot and three-foot-six-inch gauge haunt the sugar plantations of Negros Island. Many are hybridized as a result of successful cannibalization for parts. They appear as ghostlike relics – barely believable means of transport.

The locomotives are ancient, battered and often look as if they should have been abandoned centuries ago, and yet they are still running, hauling the sugar cane across the island to the crushing factories. They spark and flash across the dark nights and often even set fire to the plantations themselves, their cabs lit by the ready-made fuel of the sugar cane residues, as they haul massive weights far in excess of their intended capacities. Working on the Hawaiian Philippine Company line, these engines – most of which are Baldwin-built 0-6-0s – are known as "Dragons." They burn off the dead cane leaves after the cane has been har-

vested, to fertilize the earth in preparation for re-planting, the uncut cane still lying behind the engine's advance. The enormous tenders are stacked high with the cubes of "bagasse," the natural waste product of sugar cane processing.

These islands are like a last bastion of the very vintage steam locomotives which survive, despite all, in places like Negros – the fourth largest island in the Philippine Archepelago, which was under American rule until independence in 1946.

The huge Baldwin, four-cylinder compound 0-6-6-0 Mallet could be seen working for "Insular Lumber," a company that harvests and exports the wood of the forests. Operating out of Fabrica, in the north part of Negros Island, this incredible engine, believed to be haunted, hauled teak and mahogany from mountain stands down to the coastal saw mills. The 4-cylinder Mallet was typical but scaled down to a three-foot, six-inch gauge track. Sometimes the bridges and track areas around them look like the Old West of America, as

(Opposite)
"Dragon" number 6 – a Baldwin-built engine working the Hawaiian Philippine Sugar Company on the sugar plantations network. These engines sometimes cause fires from the sparks flying from the chimneys on the sugar cane around the tracks.

(Right)
"Dragon" number 7 – an 0-6-0 built by Baldwins during the 1920s at work on the Hawaiian Philippine system. Note the oil-burning chimney, compared with "Dragon" number 6 – opposite.

they are relics of colonial rule. In the background of these extraordinary sparking and flashing engines can be seen active volcanoes, and running behind them the mahogony-off-cut-filled tenders.

These are the last of the traditional American logging company railways on the line from the exchange sidings that then cross the Himog-an viaduct and thunder slowly to Fabrica. The viaduct has more than once burned itself down, set alight by flying and uncontrolled sparks from the chimneys of the locomotives, which very often have simply lost their spark-arresting devices.

These engines have been described as being "hideous in action and hideous in death," and to watch them crash and wobble, grind and let out their piercing, shrieking whistle sounds, is truly like watching and listening to the devil in all his glory arise out of the darkness of the forest – particularly when it happens at night.

A typhoon approaches over the Ma Ao sugar plantations as a veteran Mogul built by Alco during the 1920s sets empty king cars into a loading siding on Negros Island.

A Big Baldwin 4-cylinder compound 0-6-6-0 Mallet working for the Insular Lumbar Company in the Philippines – the engine is mahogany-burning.

An American built "Mogul" engine, stacked high with cubes of *bagasse* – used by the Ma-Ao Sugar Central on Negros Island in the Philippines.

This engine was built by Baldwins in 1925 as a 4 cylinder compound Mallet, coming to Insular Lumber in the early 40s – the locals believe it to be haunted as it has been responsible for many deaths – the sounds that it emits may account for this belief.

VIII

ASIA

A lively scene in China of an **RM** class Pacific – the most recent Pacific type in China – on a railway system that runs steam and diesel alongside one another and is still building new steam traction every year.

I N China steam is well-established and considered an efficient method of railway transportation. The improvements and redesign work are minimal, and there seems to be an understanding in this country of what the genre can do for industry and passenger work. Spare parts are very straightforward and simply acquired, and the Chinese believe in standardization, easy maintenance and making sure that their engineers are familiar with the engines. The Chinese in fact believe that a little bit of care and attention is worth more than the minimal efficiency produced by the diesel alternatives. In Tangshan even complete rebuilding of steam locomotive works were undertaken after the major earthquake in 1976, when much of the city was raized to the ground, including the steam locomotive works. Once again Tangshan produces the magnificent SY Mikados – seen on these pages – for industrial use. The engines are thoroughly tested over twenty miles on the main line, and then return to the shed for modification before final testing run.

Once the engine is finally proven, it is handed over to the operating

CHINA

authorities, who then tow them in freight trains to the industry where they have been allocated, such as the docks, coalmines, ironstone mines, or any other facet of heavy industry connected to China's national railway.

Brand new QJ type locomotives are produced in this way also at the Datong Works. Three new ones are built each week right now, and these particular engines form the principle type in China with several thousand in service. Recently, a modified version – essentially a new class – has been designed based on the QJ, the original QJ model having been in operation throughout China for thirty years.

The QJ class 2-10-2s can be seen on the main lines through Manchuria from Harbin to Pekin. Watching scenes in this part of China brings home just how virile main-line steam can be when at its height of capacity as it is in China, with the engines filtering through the coaling, watering and ash-making processes. Work is carried out round the clock, as locomotives are put back into service as quickly as possible to make use of their much-needed tasks on this potent system.

Chanchun is on China's busiest steam main line, with at least fifty QJ's,
twenty JF class Mikados and eight RM Pacifics in action at any one time.
Other types can be seen here also, mostly in derelict condition and
representing many countries of origin, such as Russia, America, Japan and
Belgium.

The lines from Chanchun go north to Harbin and south to Shenyang on
the old Manchurian main line, in addition there is a busy line to Jillin.

China has to be one of the finest train-watching countries in the world,
with the astonishing San Kong bridge in Harbin in the north east, a bridge
that overlooks the yard from which south-bound trains depart, heading
down the line to Chanchun and Shenyang – the busiest steam-worked railway in the world.

But there is one feature of the Chinese plans for their railways which does
not entirely fit with the steam lovers' pleasure at seeing engines on track –
the standardization consequence. Within China there are some eleven thousand engines altogether in the steam sector of the railway system. (Incidentally in England, at the height of British steam there were some thirty thou-

(Opposite)
A China Railways SY class 2-8-2 number 1480 brand new in the steam testing shed at Tangshan in 1986.

(This page)
China's railways are a magnificent example of a country making use of a system that works – their steam railways both in passenger service and freight operate throughout the country. The largest marshaling yards in the world still operating steam are at Manchuria.

(Opposite)
A QJ as it leaves Harbin marshaling yards in Manchuria to begin a long climb to the summit at Wang Gang. It is mechanically stoked and capable of between 2000 and 3000 ton hauls, sometimes on the climbs with double-headers.

(Right)
The famous S160 2-8-0, American-built engine, made for wartime use in Europe.

sand engines in regular use – a country that is way smaller than China today, with far smaller areas to cover and far fewer people. China has the largest population in the world – one quarter of humanity – and England then had only some sixteen million people to its name!)

Of these eleven thousand steam engines in China there are only four major groups of engine types operating – and these tend to be the simpler and more hardy designs, thus leaving a state of affairs that continually decreases the imaginative aspect of steam railway. It seems possible that pretty soon, even here in China, the diesel and electrification systems will grow larger and the steam smaller so that the varieties of design will be reduced still further.

This is one of the saddest aspects of working steam in the twentieth century, and although it is probable that steam in countries like China will go through into the twenty-first century, it appears that very soon the whole of steam heritage will have become considerably less exciting than it was in its former years.

The whole concept of steam in China is related to efficiency, and in some ways the only reason why they retain it is because they consider using what

(Right)
A QJ 2-10-2 in Harbin, taken in 1984.

(Opposite left)
A scene from San Kong Bridge in Harbin, Manchuria, in winter, with a QJ 2-10-2 China Railways engine backing onto a south-bound freight train. On the right is a JF 2-8-2.

(Opposite right)
Also San Kong Bridge which overlooks the yards from which the south-bound trains emerge.

is available more important than wasting extra resources on new design simply for the sake of appearance. Steam therefore fits. Unfortunately the way it fits does not particularly gladden the hearts of the steam enthusiast, and a certain sense of apprehension accompanies the progress there.

Calcutta, India at the great steam sheds in Howrah operating XC class Pacifics alongside British-built 0-6-0s used for mixed traffic work.

TRAVELING IN INDIA IS an incredible and fascinating experience – not to say chaotic, dirty and noisy, but one which should not be missed by the lover of steam locomotion. Of course, the Indian continent is full of steam power, working and performing like nowhere else in the world, with engines that have been maintained for half a century and longer in an environment which still genuinely needs it.

This is typified by the great sheds at Howrah near Calcutta which until recently saw XC class Pacifics resplendent in green livery, boiling up alongside British-built inside-cyclinder 0-6-0s that were used for mixed traffic work.

One of the most famous locomotive designs of all time is the XB Pacific type 99, built between 1927 and 1931, and created for medium-range express passenger work. The last survivors of this type worked from Rajamundry shed in Andra Pradesh. The XB-Cs formed part of the X series of British design for India and were intended to cope with India's inferior

INDIA

coal, having a special wide fire box. The XBs were something of a disappointment to the railway authorities, as a major derailment in 1937 caused many deaths. The findings of the investigators after the accident were that a design fault concerning the leading bogey and rear truck caused the engine to derail.

Modifications were carried out, but the XB was never again trusted with high speed work. The accompanying pictures show these thoroughbreds ending their days around the coastal regions of Andra Pradesh.

Another interesting development in steam is the use of one of the world's last steam cranes which can be found in extensive application in India – built by Manning Wardle of Leeds in 1903.

Built for a five-foot, six-inch gauge, with a twelve-by-eighteen-inch cylinder, the crane is still in use three quarters of a century later in its unchanged condition. Its work includes carrying timber into a sawmill for cutting into sleeper lengths for use on India's mainlines. Before the engine arrived in 1903 the work was done by elephants.

(Opposite and right)
One of India's magnificent British designs of the 1920s was the XD freight hauling 2-8-2s which formed part of the famous X series standards built by Britain for the 5ft 6in gauge lines of India.

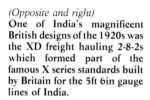

Steam cranes were an evolutionary offshoot from the conventional steam locomotion and were usually confined to iron and steel works or shipyards and marine engine works, or for use in railway main yards around workshops.

Nowadays, of course, they have been superseded by diesel cranes and heavy duty fork-lift trucks. Some two hundred and twenty of the steam cranes were built in England between 1866 and 1950.

India is an extraordinary country in every aspect of its operation, its people and its landscape, but one of its greatest problems is the advance of pollution – the arrangements for clean air and facilities are not exactly progressing. Visiting Bombay, perhaps through the Ghats and down into the outer regions of the city, is an alarming experience: some ten miles outside, there is a visible black cloud of dirt that seems today to hang permanently over the skyline. The black is of course made up largely of truck fumes and burning factory waste which climbs readily into the sky from the many chimneys that rise above the ground. However, one aspect of pollution must be the steam engine railway lines which contribute their share of dirt and soot.

An ex-World War I Baldwin 4-6-0T surviving on sugar plantation service in northern India.

A super fast suburban/cross-country 2-8-4T built by Indian Railways as their WT class in service at Rajamundry in Andhra Pradesh.

An example of the famous X series built for the 5ft 6in gauge during the 1920s – later to prove the mainstay of Indian motive power. Engine number 22543 was built for the heavy mixed traffic work. This page shows an Indian XE, 2-8-2 under attack by the demolition gangs – heavy, hard work.

A Kitson 0-6-2 of 1900 ends its days on the sugar fields of northern India.

A British-built inside-cylinder 0-6-0 at work on the Punjab of Pakistan.

THE LEGENDARY PASSION for travel that exists in India also applies to Pakistan – figures are less available but the situation is relatively the same. In India the railways carry ten million passengers a day, and this results, quite naturally, in the need to book ahead for a train ride.

A steam-hunting journey in Pakistan is an experience to remember. Starting, for example, at Karachi, an eight-hour diesel trip will bring you to the Kotri Junction opposite Hyderabad where steam takes effect. In the shunting yards of Indus can be found British BESA 2-8-0s, of clean and well-maintained appearance – much as they would have been in the 1920s. Seen in action there might also be the "Derby" – 0-6-0 BESA.

In Pakistan there is also one-meter gauge line in operation at Mirpur Khas where a pilot BESA 2-8-0 operates the broad gauge line and a 4-6-0 series deal with the meter gauge lines. Numerous other engines such as various old 4-6-0s and BESA HG 2-8-0s man the sheds in this part of the country.

PAKISTAN

But of all the Pakistan railway areas the very best for steam locomotion is at Malakwal where, at the right time of the year when the light is good, some magnificent examples can be found. As many as ten BESA 4-4-0s, as many IRS XA 4-6-2s and maybe twelve BESA 0-6-0s. Such a shed can keep an enthusiast busy for several days and the 4-4-0s are unique here – they cannot be found in working condition anywhere else in the world.

Pakistan also offers the excitement of local tribal conditions where law is interpreted according to whether you have a rifle or not, enthusiasts expecting to photograph everything might think twice before raising the camera.

With the political situation growing increasingly uncertain between the borders of Pakistan and India, the general conditions of the country do not give too much promise for improvement in certain outlying areas, particularly where tribal warfare is active. Unfortunately it is often in these remote parts of the world that the most extraordinary engines can be found. The drivers, who will sometimes be tribal members themselves, may also choose

A inside-cylinder 4-4-0 – the classic express passenger engine of late Victorian Britain, active today on cross-country services in Pakistan.

to stop the engine for a reunion with their family or friends, leaving the passengers waiting, the foreigners, especially, in a position to wish they had remained on the commuter line between New York and New Jersey!

Pakistan may appear to be similar to India in many respects, particularly the appearance of the people, but in so many other ways it is not at all similar, particularly today where internal and international conditions are altering fast. Right now the camera is almost as dangerous as the gun in any area that is associated with war or potential conflict. In this sense Pakistan is rather like the Central African countries during times of upheaval. Better to behave well and keep the camera in your bag!

However, the Pakistan Railway system is very well attended and a good deal more comfortable than any African equivalent – there will always be too many people aboard the train but at least there is some opportunity for higher class travel, as the Pakistan people operate their railways in the same way as the Indian – with various first, second and third class conditions of railway carriage.

IX

SOUTH AMERICA

One of the Teresa Cristina Railways 2-6-6-0 4-cylinder simple Mallets, Baldwin-built during the 1950s, highballs through a verdant landscape near Tubarao.

U NTIL RECENT YEARS South America was host to some of the world's most fascinating steam survivors. But today many line closures have taken place in favor of long-distance road and air transportation. In addition dieselization has been widespread over the last two decades, and although a fascinating variety of steam traction survives it is thinly spread over a vast area of the continent.

One example is a delightful narrow-gauge railway of two foot, six inches, with the network centering on Sao Joao del Rei in the Brazilian state of Minas Gerais. Here there is a stud of Baldwins ranging from 4-4-0s, 4-6-0s and 2-8-0s – all of which were originally built between 1889 and 1920. Out of Sao Joao del Rei, the system is all steam, vintage American railroad, and marvelously maintained from local resources. No diesel could ever survive so long on such a decrepit system, and it is only because of this pride in the value and excellence of the job to be done, the punctuality and cleanliness of the trains, that this railway manages to continue.

More American super-power works on the Teresa Cristina Railway in Bra-

BRAZIL

zil, operating the Texas type locomotive built during the 1940s by Baldwin and Alco. America was building 2-10-4 Texas type engines in the 1920s, when the railways of Germany were still creating 2-8-0s and 2-10-0s. Britain had barely aspired to a 2-8-0.

These giant Texas type engines could operate on the meter-gauge tracks with eighteen-hundred-ton trains almost half-a-mile long at speed of fifty miles per hour. They were magnificent machines which traversed the landscape issuing heads of steam like creatures from some mythological tale.

Other engines to be found in South America include the traditional Scottish "Pug" – a little tanker that used to shunt in many of the goods yards. Strictly speaking, a Pug is an 0-4-0, but the term became applied to Scottish shunting tanks of the six-wheel variety also. This one was manufactured at Sharp Stewart & Co. at the Atlas Works in Glasgow in 1903 for a five-foot, six-inch gauge, and now works at the Cosim steel plant near Sao Paolo, Brazil.

(Opposite)
Brazil's vastness has always required considerable railway usage – with great areas that can simply never be reached because of tropical forest regions. Engines such as the American 0-6-2 saddle tanker on this page were built for the wide gauge 5ft 6in, in 1896 – for heavy shunting.

(Right)
One of the world's last Texas type 2-10-2s on the Teresa Cristina system.

Of course, like many places in the world, extra work has been done on South American engines to improve or simply adapt their performances, and the Scottish-built Pug is no exception – for example, the water and coal bunkers capacities have been extended, as when they were delivered they were much smaller.

Many of these adaptations could almost have happened in the local blacksmith's shop!

Such engines can be seen there working in companion with two Baldwin 0-6-2 Saddle Tanks from Philadelphia, built in 1896 – classic American switchers of their period (left).

One of the main industries in Brazil, of course, is the cane sugar industry, and steam locomotion is still in use today within some plantations, and between them and the areas that mill the sugar.

An engine that will be found hauling the cane at, for example, Usina Outeiro in Brazil, is the Philadelphia-built 2-8-0 from Baldwin's works, built in 1894. This example of American design was being built in large numbers in the 1890s, long before such engines were commonplace in Britain. The

A Sharp Stewart 4-4-0 built in Glasgow in 1892 on sugar plantation service.

A scene in Tubarao depicting an array of smoky giants of classic American appearance scaled down to meter gauge proportions for operating Brazil's Teresa Cristina line.

A pair of abandoned German-built industrial locomotives lying in the old depot yard at a Paraguayan sugar factory.

cabs were beautifully designed in wood – a fine American feature – with louvered windows and incorporating a front door that opens out onto the running plate which is raised high above the driving wheels. Each cylinder is cast with half of the smoke box, and the protrusion stays for reinforcement with rectangular valve chests above the cylinder and stove-pipe chimney, followed by the sand dome behind, closer to the fire box. This contrasted with the British system in which the sand domes would rarely be carried up on the boiler, and the frames would have been of plate variety, with the cylinder cast separately without support stays. British engines of this period had lower running plates, with a metal cab and wheel splashers on the engine.

So these engines in South America used today are thoroughbred American, which were not built in any way for industrial use but for main line, later pensioned off to the industrial environments. In Paraguay at Tebicuary, on the line from Asuncion to Encarnacion it was possible to find a stud of fine old locomotives which were formerly in use on the plantation.

Sadly, the manager of the plantation, in his wisdom, decided that trucks were more efficient for bringing the cane in from the fields, and the railway network was closed and the delightful little industrial engines put out to grass. It is still possible to see these "Hanomag" 0-4-0s built in 1906 rotting away in the abandoned works. Now the only likelihood for their survival is that they are sold by the plantation for preserved lines. An example of these engines may be seen on page 242.

Pages 245 and 247 show a scene on the wood-burning, all-steam, international main line from Paraguay's capital of Asuncion to Encarnacion on the border with Argentina. From here the railway network runs to the coast at Buenos Aries via Argentina's Urquiza railway, and is standard-gauge throughout. The engine is number 152, and named "Asuncion," built in England by the Yorkshire Engine Company at its Meadowhall Works in Sheffield in 1953. The locomotive is an updated version of Paraguay's Edwardian moguls built by the North British Locomotive Co. in Glasgow.

PARAGUAY

(Right)
A picture from the most remarkable surviving railway in the world on the Paraguay line from Asuncion to the port of Encarnacion on the borders of Argentina. All the engines are wood burners and throw showers of crimson embers into the air sometimes as high as 70 feet.

(Opposite)
The remains of a Kitson-Meyer 0-6-6-0T at Taltal.

It is possible that the two remaining examples in Paraguay are the only ones left in commercial service in the world. This particular one looks entirely British in its design and manufacture, but in fact was built in Berlin.

We have spent some time in this book discussing the steam graveyards that existed in Greece, and how the whole era of steam is relegated to "cemeteries" before finally being cut up and disposed of. But South America forms a unique world locality for steam locomotive remains. If, as an enthusiast, the reader manages to pluck up the courage to travel into the tropical forests of this rich and fertile region of the world, given enough time and energy he will find some of the most amazing graveyards anywhere. The death knoll areas do not generally contain large numbers of locomotives, but single examples cast aside in the midst of the most dramatic and amazing foliage, lying like discarded skeletons, overgrown and sometimes extremely evocative, right there where they were abandoned years ago.

The advantage of this phenomenon, at least to the observer, is that to cut up and take away the old locomotives is sometimes impractical, and some are very likely to remain where they are until the end of time, or when they

(Right)
"Acuncion," a 2-6-0 built by the
Yorkshire Engine Company
during the 1950s at work in
Paraguay.

(Opposite)
"Laurita," an 0-6-0WT built by
Arthur Koppel in Berlin, at
work on a lumbar line in
Paraguay.

finally rot to disintegration or become buried by so much forestry foliage
that they are invisible. Perhaps in centuries to come, when man has finally
forgotten what steam locomotion was like, examples from these remaining
graveyards will be dug up as symbols to future generations of a vast epoch
– somewhat as the woolly mammoth was when uncovered amid the frozen
vastness of Siberia.

For those who have not visited any South American country, the trip may
be expensive, but the experience will be worthwhile. The most important
feature within this often untamed continent is that vast areas of the land simply cannot be crossed by normal transportation. Jungle covers the greater
part of countries like Brazil so that getting from one place to another is frequently hazardous. The necessity to be prepared for a hard ride becomes evident the moment the visitor arrives.

However, compared to much of the rest of the world, South America is
largely as it was when, in Europe and the US, steam locomotion was still running "full steam." A direct experience of what it is like to participate in a
steam operated railway network can still be enjoyed there.

Here on the 5ft 6in lines of Argentina is another typical British inside-cylinder 0-6-0 shunting tank, which the Argentinians classify as BE. It has 16in x 24in cylinders and coupled wheels of 4ft 1in diameter.

In Argentina today, there is little steam in regular service. Latter day operations, however, included marvelous "Prairie" 2-6-2 oil burners in service on Argentina's General Belgrano meter-gauge network (pages 250 and 251). Very often, as in other countries, steam locomotives such as this one, are used to retrieve broken-down diesels – again exemplifying the superior staying power of steam.

The 10A class of the Belgrano Railway was originally wood-burning, and constructed in Switzerland in 1909, converted to oil and allocated to Sante Fe in Argentina. It is here that the main workshops are situated with one of the largest shed buildings in the country, having stalls and room for fifty locomotives under cover.

In 1948 Argentina nationalized its railway system, and within the Sante Fe shed one hundred and forty-four engines were allocated. This indicates an incredible steam railway heritage on both broad and meter-gauge systems within the country.

ARGENTINA

Argentina's railways embrace several different gauges, and the vast majority of the country's network was British-built. In common with India, Argentina's railways mirrored those of the mother country more than any other. Passenger trains were fast, efficient and punctual, whilst a phenomenal tonnage of freight was also handled. It is no exaggeration to say that Argentina's railways made the country the bread-basket of the world by moving huge amounts of grain and meat to the ports on the Atlantic coast, and the inter-war years pushed Argentina's economy to global pre-eminence. Today, road transport is tragically taken more seriously than railways, and most of the classic steam designs are no more. Owing to the running down of the system their diesel counterparts are doing an inferior job. One marvelous Argentinian survivor is the steam tram, two examples of which were sold by the Municipality of Buenos Aires and pensioned off to the sugar plantations in neighboring Paraguay and now work for the sugar factory at Tebicuary, alongside the standard-gauge, all-steam main line. The trams

(This page and opposite right) A 2-6-2 type "Prairie" from a batch built for the meter gauge of the Santa Fe Railway of Argentina between 1909 and 1911. They are the last of their type.

One of the world's last 3-cylinder locomotives at work in Argentina. She is an 11C class 4-8-0 of classic 1920s British styling.

A very rare engine – 38 class 4-6-0, ten-wheeler made in America. Here she is shunting at the San Bernardo works in the morning, and in the afternoon she transferred to a passenger line pulling antiquated coaches.

bring train loads of sugar out of the factory and place them on the connection to the main line train, which then runs along the international main line from Paraguay's capital to Buenos Aires in Argentina.

The steam tram is now almost extinct, though it forms another fascinating variation on the conventional locomotive.

As a final word, to round off this book, South America's dying heritage of steam forms the end of a natural circle of events. Steam began in England and America with much resistence and many problems. First the skeptics and adversaries of the new industrial force had to be overcome, then came the engineering problems, the land problems, and the economics of creating something so ambitious and different – all these things were faced and surmounted before railway ever managed to make its mark on the world.

Once the whole effort had reached a peak of energy and the steam locomotives had proven their immense capacity to change the world, the story began to take a turn for the better; the process of improvement, streamlining,

CHILE

extra speed, comfort and power made their mark also, so that railway transport became a matter of accepted style and usefulness. Around the end of the nineteenth century and before World War I railway transport was a norm and seemed only to be available for better and better results. But, as with many technological innovations, there is a peak point at which man becomes aware that if he can go this far, then perhaps there are alternative ways he can go further still. Coal resources had been attacked so violently throughout the world that the quality of this natural fuel was deteriorating. As steam power relies heavily on coal – wood-burning could never be as successful – then the drop in coal quality meant a drop in enthusiasm for this transport system. Electricity had, in the early part of the century, become a phenomenon of equal interest to the phenomenon of steam during the nineteenth century. Electricity was clean, more available, more adaptable and tied very closely in with other innovations such as communication, heating and comfort. The development of diesel, right or wrong, was as natural as that of steam and, unfortunately – though it might not appeal to the steam

(Opposite and right)
The front chimney is issuing shrouds of dark oil smoke, while the rear chimney issues pure white saturated steam. The front pair of cylinders exhaust their steam plus the gases from the fire. This number 59 lingered on at Taltal, being engaged in demolition work of the once vast nitrate railways in Chile.

engine enthusiast – there is no way that steam locomotion can co-exist for long with the power and efficiency of electricity.

In South America, the glamor, glory and romance of steam locomotion remains as evidence of an era that made man's existence the more enticing and left proof of his immense capability for pioneering and improving his world.

Without it, the past and parts of the present would be far less admirable.

Aknowledgements.

The Publishers wish to acknowledge the following for the right to use their photographs and illustrations in this book:
AFE - Piero Servo - Rome, Italy - p. 19
Association of American Railroads - p. 22
Bledsoe Rail Slides - pp. 24, 25, 30, 31.
D-Day Agency - Padua, Italy - pp. 61, 64, 68, 70, 73, 76, 77, 78, 120, 121, 122, 124, 125, 126, 127, 128, 129, 130, 131, 132, 134, 135, 136, 137, 138, 139, 144, 154, 155, 156, 157, 160, 161, 162, 164, 165, 167, 168, 169, 179, 181, 216, 217.
Edaville Railroad - p. 26
Colin Garratt Archives - pp. 41, 43, 45, 46, 50, 51, 52, 53, 54, 56, 57, 98, 112, 113, 114, 115, 116, 118, 140, 141, 143, 145, 146, 148, 150, 151, 152, 158, 159, 163, 166, 170, 171, 172, 173, 174, 176, 178, 180, 182, 183, 184, 185, 186, 188, 190, 192, 194, 196, 197, 198, 200, 201, 206, 208, 209, 210, 211, 212, 213, 214, 218, 219, 220, 221, 222, 223, 224, 226, 227, 228, 229, 230, 231, 232, 234, 236, 238, 239, 240, 241, 242, 244, 245, 246, 247, 248, 250, 251, 252, 254, 255.
Gulf Oil Company Inc. - p. 19.
Tom Haraden - p. 16.
Anthony J. Lambert - pp. 13, 20, 21, 28, 32, 33, 38, 39.
K.P. Lawrence - pp. 202, 204.
National Railway Museum - p. 40.
Richard Steinheimer - p. 27.
J. Winkley - pp. 5, 8, 12, 36, 37, 42, 44, 48, 49, 60, 64, 71, 72, 79, 80, 82, 83, 84, 85, 86, 88, 90, 92, 93, 96, 99, 100, 102, 103, 104, 105, 106, 107, 108, 109, 110, 111.